Praise for

SIPPING DOM PÉRIGNON THROUGH A STRAW

"Eddie Ndopu is a brilliant, courageous and imaginative soul with the kind of conviction that can change the world. We will all benefit from his story." **—Imani Perry, National Book Award winning author of** *South to America*

"With nflinching honesty and vulnerability, Ndopu's jaw-dropping story serves as a clarion call for a more inclusive and compassionate world. Prepare to be moved, enlightened, and profoundly touched by the extraordinary life and wisdom of Eddie Ndopu." **—Sabrina Dhowre Elba, actress, model, and UN Goodwill Ambassador**

"*Sipping Dom Pérignon Through a Straw* not only highlights the injustices and dehumanization that disabled people face daily, but illuminates the need for amplifying disabled voices and disabled self-advocacy. Eddie's radical transparency about his triumphs in the face of lifelong systemic oppression is profound." **—Blair Imani, educator and author of** *Read This to Get Smarter*

SIPPING
DOM PÉRIGNON
THROUGH A STRAW

SIPPING DOM PÉRIGNON THROUGH A STRAW

Reimagining Success as a Disabled Achiever

EDDIE NDOPU

Written Entirely Using My One Good Finger

LEGACY
LIT

NEW YORK BOSTON

Legacy Lit, an imprint of Hachette Books
Hachette Book Group
1290 Avenue of the Americas
New York, NY 10104
LegacyLitBooks.com
Twitter.com/LegacyLitBooks
Instagram.com/LegacyLitBooks

First Edition: August 2023

Grand Central Publishing is a division of Hachette Book Group, Inc. Legacy Lit is an imprint of Grand Central Publishing. The Legacy Lit and Grand Central Publishing names and logos are trademarks of Hachette Book Group, Inc.

The publisher is not responsible for websites (or their content) that are not owned by the publisher.

The Hachette Speakers Bureau provides a wide range of authors for speaking events.
To find out more, go to hachettespeakersbureau.com or email HachetteSpeakers@hbgusa.com.

Library of Congress Cataloging-in-Publication Data has been applied for.

ISBN: 9780306829062 (hardcover), 9780306829086 (ebook)

Printed in the United States of America

LSC

Printing 1, 2023

A toast: Here's to my beloved brother, Wonga, and to all my siblings with disabilities around the world. Let's raise a glass in celebration of our magnificence. Cheers!

"I want to live the rest of my life, however long or short, with as much sweetness as I can decently manage, loving all the people I love, and doing as much as I can of the work I still have to do. I am going to write fire until it comes out of my ears, my eyes, my noseholes—everywhere. Until it's every breath I breathe. I'm going to go out like a fucking meteor!"

—AUDRE LORDE

SIPPING
DOM PÉRIGNON
THROUGH A STRAW

PROLOGUE

I HAD BECOME NOTHING more than a chore to my new
care aide, Six. Merely a task to be ticked off on a checklist.
Like the five others before him one of his deliverables was
to shower me. Carefully, Six turned the faucet and, at first, a
weak stream of water sputtered out of the showerhead. However, it didn't take long for the water to become a steady flow.
As I sat there on the commode chair, I watched as Six's arm
parted the running water to gauge the temperature. Given my
fondness for steamy showers, we had to wait an extra minute
or so for the boiler to rouse from its slumber. Although the
building in which we found ourselves was the newest addition on the Somerville premises, the plumbing system was a
testament to Oxford's venerable age. Indeed, even Oxford's

fabled cobblestone walkways were laid down far before the world as we know it had taken shape.

As I waited, I struggled to keep my yawning at bay. Frankly, I could have benefited from another hour or two of sleep to bolster my endurance for the long day of back-to-back lectures and extracurricular activities that awaited me. Alas, bone-piercing exhaustion had now become a defining feature of my student life. I was used to operating on empty.

Six lowered his arm and flicked the water off of his fingertips, a sign that the temperature was perfect. He wheeled me into the shower. As soon as the warm water enveloped me, it felt like a moment of refuge from the world and its lack of concern for the pressures that had made it difficult for me to get a good night's sleep. Under the water, the constant chatter in my mind was silenced, offering a brief but welcome respite from the anxiety of having to raise £80,000 in a matter of weeks to pay for my care, which included the premium cost of Six's services. With my eyes closed, I savored each moment before having to deliver a speech that morning to finalize my run for student body president and make a case to the Oxford officials that I was worth the investment.

Six lumped a cold gooey blob of shampoo on top of my head. As he lathered and massaged the soapy gel through my hair and onto my scalp, his stubby fingers brushed past an itchy spot. Before I could direct him to the site of my sudden urge to be scratched, a siren unceremoniously went off.

"Jesus," I exclaimed, taken aback. Then I remembered

seeing an email from the college's facilities manager earlier in the week, informing students of a scheduled fire drill. "Oh, don't worry. That's just the fire drill. Let's continue," I said, trying to speak through the shampoo in my eyes.

Six abruptly turned off the water.

"What are you doing?" I asked, surprised.

"I have to take you outside," he replied, unperturbed.

"But we're still in the middle of my shower."

"The facilities manager told me that I have to take you outside immediately whenever I hear the fire alarm," he explained, beginning to wheel me out of the shower.

"No, wait," I said. "Why don't you go outside and explain to him that I am in the middle of a shower? It will still take you some time to get me dressed. See if you can get him to let us continue." I was sure that my request was reasonable. After all, my living quarters were designed to be inclusive, and I assumed that protocols could be adjusted to accommodate my needs. Even if it wasn't, though, I'd assumed that Six would have at the very least sought my consent first before yanking me out like this.

Six grabbed the towel that hung from the railing against the wall and dabbed my small, nude frame, doubling down on his disregard for my autonomy. Befuddled by the fluidity, certainty, and intentionality of his movements, I considered the possibility that perhaps he hadn't heard me clearly, so I repeated myself. But he looked right through me. Then he reached for the cabinet under the sink and retrieved another towel, the biggest one I had, and draped it over the front of my body. "Let's go," he said. I chuckled, convinced that this was a prank. *There's no way he'd ignore me,* I thought. *Surely he wouldn't do that.* It was only when he parked me in the doorway and circled his way around me to open the front door that I realized that Six was dead serious.

"I can't go out like this," I protested. "I still have shampoo in my hair." I was so utterly perplexed by this intransigent behavior that the incessant stinging in my eyes eclipsed the issue of my nakedness. He wheeled me farther until we spilled out into the hallway of the dormitory. I couldn't tell if the corridor was empty because all the other students had already bolted out of their rooms or if, because of Six's zombie-like embrace of institutional authority, I had beaten them all to it. Whatever the reason, no one was immediately there to bear witness to my forced removal. "You're not serious! Please take me back," I pleaded, defenseless.

"We can't break the rules," Six said, breaking his silence to stun me into one of my own. I couldn't recall ever feeling more violated. My own body had suddenly become unspeakable. I found myself sinking to the bottom of a visceral culmination of all the harrowing things I had gone through over the last twelve weeks of my new academic life. I thought to myself, *How the fuck did I get here?*

Six swerved the commode chair to the left, rendering me powerless and emotionally drained in my seat. He charged straight down the hallway, propelling me toward the building's main entrance, which opened up into the concourse where roll call was going to be taken. He pushed me through the doorway, down the slope, and around the corner, where a small group of students sat huddled together on the ground, awaiting further instructions. To compound matters, I spotted some of my classmates trickling in, classmates who I would soon have to face in my bid for student body president in the coming hours. They looked cozy and comfortable, wrapped up in fleece pajamas and woolen morning gowns while I shivered under a bath sheet that offered little protection from the bitter morning wind. Go figure. I was still naked.

The chill that coursed through me wasn't just from the cold. I knew that for my upright, non-wheelchair-using counterparts this fire drill was but a minor annoyance, as they could easily make up for lost time. However, for me—a nonupright—this was a massive disruption to my morning routine, which was a complex and fixed operation that began before dawn each day. Six was well aware of this.

I had come to Oxford to bolster my credentials with an advanced degree from the world's leading university. Yet here I was, a human rights practitioner, at the receiving end of such apparent disregard for my own rights. Cold and sobered, I dispelled any notion that my achievements would somehow inoculate me against ableism.

I couldn't help but feel I was still merely seen as a "cripple."

Feeling crestfallen and humiliated, I couldn't help but contemplate the injustice of it all. As I gazed out onto the manicured grounds, I had to come to terms with the harsh reality that Oxford might never validate me in the way I hoped it would. Just when I thought my graduate experience couldn't get any worse, I was now struggling to hold back tears, while Six—whom I'd entrusted with my well-being, from personal hygiene to my feeding and more—stood on the sideline, with his arms crossed in detectable callous detachment.

ONE

IT WAS A MID-SEPTEMBER EVENING, and the South African winter had made a final, fleeting return, driving spring into hiding. But within the walls of my friend Thandie's opulent penthouse, overlooking the sprawling Johannesburg skyline, there was no lack of warmth to be found. Thandie, a petite yet vivacious news broadcaster, was hosting a dinner party that promised to be the talk of the town. Afro-jazz melodies wafted through the air as guests mingled and conversed.

As the atmosphere grew increasingly relaxed, Thandie plucked a fork from the tray of canapés offered by the caterer and gently clinked her champagne flute, still clutched in her other hand. "Gather 'round, friends," she proclaimed, commanding the attention of the room. "I would like to offer a toast to our guest of honor." With a playful wink in my direction, she gestured for me to join her at the front of the room. "Come, come, come," she coaxed.

I flicked my joystick, guiding my wheelchair forward. Then I executed a smooth 180-degree turn as I approached Thandie. In a maneuver akin to parallel parking, I backed into place beside her, taking stock of the diverse and captivating crowd before me: septum nose rings glinting, henna tattoos on display, kente cloth overlaid with sequins, crisp white shirts and embroidered head wraps, towering platform heels. Thandie placed a delicate hand on my shoulder as she proudly raised her glass.

"Let us raise a toast to our dear friend and brother, Eddie Ndopu, for making history as the first disabled Black man to be accepted into the Masters in Public Policy program at Oxford University."

As Thandie's words washed over me, I was transported back to a lovely interview between Toni Morrison and Oprah Winfrey, in which Winfrey asked the legendary author how she felt upon learning of her Nobel Prize for Literature win as the first Black woman to receive the award. Morrison's response was unforgettable: "Now is not the time to be humble." Her words echoed in my mind, and I found myself channeling her unbridled confidence in that moment, basking in the applause and adulation of my friends and peers.

"Eddie," Thandie said, turning to face me with a serene smile. "Do you remember the day you got the news?"

"Oh my God, yes," I said, face flushed. "But please don't recount this story. I'm such a drama queen."

Sipping Dom Pérignon Through a Straw

"You know I don't have a problem making you blush, darling, so I'm gonna go ahead and share this with all of you," Thandie cackled. "So when I arrived home from work one afternoon, I found Eddie sitting in my living room, alone. You know, to this day, I still don't know why you were sitting by yourself, darling. Lucky, you weren't doing your job," she joked, locking eyes with my care aide, Lucky, who was standing off to the side, holding my drink in his hand. "Anyway, I see Eddie staring at the TV screen, which was off, and I'm like, 'Is this man okay?' So I walk over to him and ask if he's all right. He doesn't say a word. Now I'm starting to think something is seriously wrong."

I chuckled softly. Thandie needn't have worried. The scene she'd walked into was simply me reflecting deeply on how far I'd come. At some point between the intermingled years of five and seven, when my family and I were still living in the arid, lackadaisical city of Windhoek, Namibia, I'd spaced out under similar conditions. The difference then was that I could still indulge in the meditative practice of dragging myself across the floor on all fours like a puppy, which was my favorite pastime growing up. One day I plonked my pudgy little body on the linoleum floor in front of the television set with my head craned up to the blank screen. My nanny was in Mom's room across the hall, cackling on the phone with what sounded like the voice of a man, barely registering my existence. Mom would eventually sack her like she'd sacked the others who'd made a habit of disappearing each time they'd collected their wages, returning days afterward with but a black eye as an explanation for their absence. A tragedy on all fronts. That evening, Mom found me spaced out in front of the screen. Even after several attempts to get me to say something, anything, I just sat there, mum, with my eyes fixed on a screen that only worked when its antenna was taped up. I didn't know how to say to her that I had been feeling unstimulated sitting at home all day in the company of a detached nanny.

More than anything in the world, I longed to be like my younger brother, Wonga, who spent his days attending school. Even though he was technically only in preschool, my developing brain didn't care about the semantics.

Whenever I accompanied Mom to pick Wonga up from school, she always asked him about his day. From his enthusiastic responses, I gathered that school was a magical place where children engaged in fun activities like learning the alphabet through song and dance, counting to ten, and befriending other kids during snack time. Wonga's stories about making friends always struck a chord, as I listened eagerly to his school day testimonials.

I was lonely. But how to say that as a child? I didn't yet have the words to articulate my isolation to Mom the day she found me stationed in front of the blank TV set. I remained that way for several more minutes, mulling over whether I should take Mom into confidence. That was until she hit the fail-safe. Mom lowered herself to my eye level and snuggled up next to me. I turned to her and broke my silence.

"Mommy, I want to go to school."

With this utterance I spoke into existence the unimaginable trajectory I have since found myself on. Mom placed all bets on me from that day onward, doing everything in her power to get me into school, not accepting no for an answer when educators and perfect strangers alike told her that it couldn't be done. The statistics were not in our favor, as the United Nations reports that only a mere fraction of children with disabilities in developing nations are able to reach their first year of schooling due to a range of factors, not least because of social stigma and structural exclusion. But my mom's determination was unbreakable, like a towering oak that refused to bend in the face of a storm. Thanks to her, that lonely child not only achieved his dream of going to school, but he wound up exceeding everyone's expectations of what was possible: becoming a poster child for the transformative power of inclusive education.

"So I sit beside him and hold his hands in my lap," Thandie continued. "Then he very calmly tells me that he just got accepted to Oxford. Cool as a cucumber. I was like, 'How are you so fucking chill about this?' Of course, at that point, I start screaming for the both of us." Thandie looked back at me. After pausing for a minute or so, she leaned in and said,

"Come to think of it, darling, you are a bit of a drama queen."
I laughed out loud. So did everyone else.

As I sat there listening to Thandie recount the day she walked in on me spacing out in her living room, I silently marked this as a full circle moment. Over the years, I had become a global advocate for the right to education. Even as a teenager, I'd appeared on television numerous times, speaking before world leaders, urging them to open up educational opportunities for children with disabilities. The statistics I'd quoted in my speeches as a campaigner in my teens remained unchanged. But here's the thing about data sets: they don't account for outliers. Every so often, the data points and hypotheses fail to capture those of us with an incalculable tenacity and will to succeed. The statistics rarely capture the real-life fightbacks waged against wider, inbuilt societal prejudices. Case in point: I went from being one of only a handful of disabled kids in Namibia to be enrolled in the country's mainstream education system in the late nineties to now joining the astonishingly small club of profoundly disabled scholars to ever be admitted to Oxford in the university's nine-hundred-plus-year history. My imminent ascension to the pinnacle of educational success was therefore not just a personal achievement but a symbolic victory for the tens of millions of kids elbowed out of the classroom. Indeed, now was not the time to be humble. This was a fucking big deal. An occasion worthy of a toast.

Sipping Dom Pérignon Through a Straw

"Eddie, darling, cheers to summiting the mountain," Thandie said. "No doubt that Oxford is the ultimate stamp of approval. I want you to remember this as you get ready to leave us next week," she said, peering down into my eyes. "You may be getting an Oxford education, but Oxford will be getting an Eddie-cation, darling, because wherever you go you always leave your mark. It's just what you do." Thandie raised her glass. "To Eddie," she toasted.

"To Eddie," echoed the entire room.

TWO

Lucky approached me with a glow of pride illuminating his features. He raised my champagne flute, the straw swaying within its bubbling contents, the gleam in his eyes seeming to refract the light that surrounded the sweating glass. As Lucky angled it to my lips, I took a sip of my signature drink and regarded him with newfound appreciation. It was as if I were seeing him for the first time, with his appearance resembling the iconic artist Jean-Michel Basquiat, save for the healthy cascade of his locks in comparison to the shock sprouting from the legendary American artist's head. My gaze traced the lines of Lucky's face, pausing on his megawatt smile before trailing down to the veins that spider-webbed across the hand that gripped the stem of the flute. In that moment, my love for him swelled to the surface, like the effervescence in my glass.

"Speech, speech, speech," chanted the room. Thandie and Lucky stood back to give me the floor.

"Um," I started, pausing to gather my thoughts. "This must be one of only a handful of occasions where I am truly at a loss for words. To be honest, none of this has sunk in yet. But I am so grateful to all of you for showing up tonight and showering me with love. I especially want to thank you, Thandie, my love, for organizing all of this and for hosting us in your beautiful home. You are the textbook definition of a friend. I adore you."

"There's one person in particular I owe a profound debt of gratitude to as I get ready to embark on this exciting journey. You, Adrian," I said, holding his gaze as he leaned against a column at the far end of the apartment. With one leg sleekly crossed over the other, Adrian was a commanding presence, a man who filled a room with his aura. His devilish good looks were almost intimidating, with chiseled features that could have made him the envy of Ralph Lauren models. His perfectly coiffed Afro had never a hair out of place, and with his athletic build, he could have easily passed off as the sixth member of the Jackson Five in another life.

As if being gifted with good genes wasn't sufficient, Adrian had also been gifted with a heart larger than most. He cheered me on before the ink had dried on the receipt of my acceptance, when my history-making admission to the oldest university in the English-speaking world was hanging in the balance. In the days following my offer of admission, I was awarded a full scholarship to secure my spot in the intensive one-year master's program at the Blavatnik School of Government. It was the icing on an already scrumptious cake.

I'd read the email several times to be absolutely sure that my tuition would be taken care of. The scholarship package even included a monthly stipend for living expenses. But despite this wonderful news, my stomach was bunched up in knots by the end of the letter. Oxford had omitted in their correspondence how they intended to support the costs associated with my disability-related needs. I'd written about my disability in my application ad nauseam, delineating on almost every page how the trials and tribulations of my life as a disabled achiever had empowered and complicated my work in human rights advocacy. I even pulled from my experiences documenting human rights abuses at Amnesty International, where I'd worked for nearly two years before applying to Oxford. I had navigated the rough terrain of the places where those atrocities occur, and that position in the driver's seat flipped the script of power relations, making me a campaigner rather than a beneficiary on the receiving end. So the school's failure to price in the lived experience my admission came with felt like dining out at a fancy restaurant and being told by the owner of the establishment that in addition to your meal you have to pay extra for the plate on which your food is served.

The omission not only left a bitter aftertaste but also made me feel unsure of how to respond.

Fortunately, Adrian came to my aid and assisted me in composing a reply. He recognized that I had already done the heavy lifting, not only throughout the application process but through my daily endurance that culminated in this moment. He understood that what I required now was institutional support, not to be left to my own devices. To the outside world, my success breaking down barriers looked effortless. As my friend, Adrian knew that outperforming my own abilities was intrinsically taxing and arduous, even when I'd made it look somewhat easy. Oxford, therefore, needed to rise to the occasion of my historic admission and meet me halfway.

Spent and indignant, I'd often found myself wondering what more I needed to do to be embraced without qualification. Why is it that as a prerequisite for our humanity to be affirmed, we as disabled people constantly find ourselves in situations where we are required to strip ourselves bare? Why are we required to overexplain, only to be underserved in turn? Uprights, a cheeky little descriptor I coined in reference to the planet's nondisabled ambulatory population, often require us to jump through hoops to get the support we need, wanting to know everything about our medical lives but nothing about the structures that impede our ability to survive in a world not built with our lived experiences in mind. We are required to exhibit the details of how we live in our bodies—what we look like naked, how we poop, whether we drool when we speak, if we can speak at all—to prove our need for institutional care. Simply accepting us at our word isn't enough for them. Yet the same is never required of uprights.

It's exhausting having to expend additional labor, especially when said labor is in psychological terms, just to be able to compete on an equal footing. That's why I needed backup. Adrian became my upright whisperer, an ally of sorts. In my reply to the university, he gave me the words to articulate what was at stake. That the funds to meet my needs—funds that technically should be viewed as an investment in talent rather than as an irregular expenditure—was the difference between successfully attending Oxford and having an artificial limit on my ability to soar because of the limitations of my body. Compelling, certainly, but the letter needed to go further to get my point across. Rather than just highlighting the funding shortfall, Adrian and I needed to provide another layer of context by spoon-feeding the nature of my existence to the admissions officers. Either that, or I risked having the "recognition" and "accommodation" of my humanity drip-fed back to me. Adrian helped me understand that this needed to be done if I wanted to cross over into a world where so few of us had been before.

I started off by thanking Oxford for awarding me such a prestigious scholarship, expressing how humbled I was by it. Then I cut to the chase by rehashing the fundamentals about my neuromuscular condition. I reminded them that despite my brilliance they were still dealing with someone who had been diagnosed with Spinal Muscular Atrophy at age two and who had been projected not to live beyond the age of five. While I continued to outlive my prognosis, my condition remained degenerative. In other words, as I spelled it out for them, my body continued to grow weaker by the year. Therefore, the logistics associated with my disability made it essential that Lucky, as my personal care aide, accompany me to Oxford for the duration of my studies. Pressing the point further, I stressed the fact that Lucky was an intimate and very literal extension of my body and that without him, I wouldn't be able to get dressed in the morning, eat in the cafeteria, get in and out of my wheelchair, or do any other physical activities of daily living for that matter. Though I hated how the fullness of my being had to be truncated and interpreted into language that appeased a world entirely centering the sensibilities of uprights, I'd come too far only for the biggest milestone of my career to wind up becoming nothing more than a damp squib. I made my ask. Based on the numbers Adrian had helped me crunch, I needed an additional £20,000 to plug the gap in my full scholarship.

Silence descended upon me, like a heavy shroud, as days turned into weeks following my letter's reception. My patience was worn thin and my anxiety reached a boiling point, leading me to take matters into my own hands. With Adrian's unwavering support and the help of my friends, I embarked on a journey to secure my place at the university through the launch of an online campaign—#OxfordEddiecated. My aim was to crowdfund the £20,000 necessary for my education.

Sipping Dom Pérignon Through a Straw

The crowdfunding drive was infused with creativity, inspired by the old adage, "When life gives you lemons, make lemonade." I instead chose to create a lemon meringue pie and incorporated a photo exhibit into the campaign. Being the showman I was, I couldn't resist the opportunity to make a statement.

On a summer's afternoon, I found myself in the back of a creaky vehicle with my entourage in tow: the photographer (a dead ringer for Lenny Kravitz), the stylist for the shoot, and the makeup artist. We roamed the streets of Johannesburg, searching for the perfect backdrop for the photoshoot, with me dressed in a voluminous purple tutu, hand-me-down Vivienne Westwood boots, and a shimmering metallic grey tank top. My hair was styled in yarn braids fashioned into an ice-cream-cone updo.

Our search led us to a park in the heart of the city, where we stumbled upon a scenic patch of land under a jacaranda tree in full bloom. It was adjacent to a dilapidated basketball court, where a group of men were playing. My entourage and I wheeled ourselves past the court, drawing the attention of the players. As I sat regally under the tree in my wheelchair, their eyes, large and piercing, looked at me admiringly, and the men shouted, "Nice fit, bro!" The photographer captured my regal pose, and I gazed down the lens with a focus that was ravenous.

The onlookers grew in number, as joggers and suburban women pushing strollers joined the amateur basketball team to bear witness to the spectacle. I basked in their gaze, looking regal and otherworldly, like the "Purple Rain" singer himself, too magnificent to be categorized or defined.

After a few more shots, I asked the photographer to show me the portraits he had taken. As he flicked through the slide-show, crouching beside me, he whispered, "There you are, the beautiful being in the purple tutu." The images behind the lens traveled to the ends of the world and not only helped attract donations to my campaign but also showcased disability in all its bedazzled, technicolor vibrancy and vitality.

"Adrian, brother, come up here," I said, summoning him from the back of Thandie's sprawling living room. As he steadily made his way through all the bodies huddled together in a warm embrace, I started tearing up. I was so grateful to have had him in my corner throughout the fundraising journey.

Several months into our campaign to get me to Oxford, we exceeded our target by almost £2,000. Around the same time, I finally heard back from the university's bureaucracy. An upright who ran the Disability Advisory Services department circled back with a lengthy email of her own. It started well enough, inquiring into the specifics of my academic accommodation needs, asking for more details about adaptive technologies like voice recognition software, and exploring whether I needed a designated notetaker during lectures to augment my learning. Crucially, she mentioned that in accordance with Oxford's collegiate system, I had been made a member of Somerville College, only a stone's throw away from the building housing the public policy program into which I was admitted. At Somerville College, I'd be accommodated in the dormitory building typically reserved for their doctoral students, as those rooms had been built with enclosed bathrooms and were generally more spacious than the standard dorms. The room that had been identified for me was apparently still being renovated, but it would be ready for me by the time I arrived for the first semester, referred to as Michaelmas term by the Oxonians. Additionally, she confirmed that the university would be able to procure a commode for me to allow me to shower. But despite these accommodations, the Oxford representative stressed that neither the university nor Somerville College was in a position to cover the cost of the most essential of my accommodation needs and the prerequisite for me to be able to enjoy all the other services they offered—a care aide. I was stunned. It didn't make any sense. Oxford's wealth, a bit like the Vatican's, was breathtaking, the stuff of which legends were made. The history of its endowment has roots in the windfalls generated from colonial conquest. That aside, this really wasn't a lot of money in institutional terms. There was no reason why they couldn't adjust my scholarship to accommodate my care costs. But whatever the reasoning behind their stinginess, I was grateful I had trusted my instincts and hadn't waited for this disappointing response before deciding to embark on a fundraising drive.

"So as some of you might remember," I recounted at the toast, "when Oxford said they couldn't top up my full scholarship, I sulked for weeks on end. I felt defeated, and come to think of it, I think I was even depressed. I believed that the universe had played a cruel prank on me for allowing my very own piece of history to slip through my fingers. But it was this man next to me who encouraged me to hold on tightly to my dream and forge ahead stridently. With Adrian's help, and thanks to the many of you in this room here tonight who contributed to #OxfordEddiecated, together we've raised £22,000 in six months. I speak for both Lucky and me when I say that we're so grateful to you guys. Oxford, here I come!" As guests hollered, whistled, howled, and applauded, I looked up at Adrian, beaming.

"Finally, and I promise I'll shut up after this," I said through scattered chuckles, "I wanna thank you, Lucky, my right-hand guy, not only for being an extension of my body but for filling my life with so much adventure. Can't wait to take Oxford by storm with you there by my side," I said, winking at him.

For the next few hours, we all mingled and nibbled on hors d'oeuvres, overjoyed to be in one another's company. Toward the end of the evening, Lucky meandered his way to the front of the room. "I think it's time we continued this party elsewhere," he announced, a declarative invitation to go clubbing that was met with a resounding cheer by everyone except Adrian. Just as he took a swig from the frosted glass in his hand, I caught Adrian rolling his eyes and snickering under his breath in response to Lucky. Pretending as though I hadn't noticed the passive aggression, I redirected my gaze to everyone else in the room.

"You better preach," Maxwell interjected. "There's a new club across the street. I went the Saturday after I flew into town and, child, when I tell you—I got my life! Best groove I've ever had in Joburg. Just as popping as my spot in the East Village," Maxwell said, as he smacked his tongue against the roof of his mouth. With his bleached-blond Afro, kind eyes, and booming voice, Maxwell's genuine love of people was a close second to his undying love for Beyoncé. Newtown, Johannesburg; Brooklyn, New York; Shoreditch, London. These were all the places Maxwell had called home in the span of two years before eventually deciding to settle in downtown Hong Kong where he was currently trying to "find himself." A trust fund kid who relished life in the fast lane, Maxwell's only real occupation was stumbling out of bars at six o'clock in the morning. He was the kind of guy for whom the walk of shame meant the strut of pride. "Y'all wanna go?" he inquired, gauging the interest.

Folks squealed with delight, as many of them looked like they weren't ready to call it a night just yet. Except for Thandie, whose eyes were bloodshot. "That's my cue," she announced, waddling over to me. She held my face in the palms of her hands and kissed my forehead goodnight. "You youngsters go. Some of us need our beauty sleep to survive."

ONE OF THE FEW PRIVILEGES I enjoyed as a young, urbane wheelchair user in their twenties was the unofficial right to skip the line. Airports, grocery stores, and coffee shops were, in this small way, my domain. It said nothing about the accessibility conditions inside the establishments, but it was a start and admittedly pretty sweet. When we arrived at the establishment Maxwell had recommended, I led the crew straight to the front, whooshing past the other partygoers languishing in line. "We're all together," I said, as I craned my head up to make eye contact with the bouncer. He glanced down at our IDs, gave us a stoic nod, and retracted the barrier belt to let us in. We scuttled our way through a grimy, unlit passage, stopping along the way to check our coats, together with our inhibitions and dignity. From there, we followed the music, which intensified the closer we got to the dance floor. The combined whiff of sweat, liquor, and smoke greeted us as we rounded the corner. While the rest of the crew dispersed and disappeared into the debaucherous distance, Lucky, Adrian, and Maxwell remained by my side and formed a barrier around me to stop the uprights—who looked stunned to see a wheelchair user in their midst (because, you know, disabled people evaporate at night)—from colliding into me as I

navigated their flailing limbs. It was a relief when I successfully found my way to a booth where I could catch my breath
and bob my head to the beat in peace.

At some point, between the time Adrian left to get drinks
and when my song request made the cut, I turned my head to
find Maxwell mounted against a wall with his legs wrapped
around Lucky's waist as they slurped each other's faces. I
couldn't take my eyes off of them, and yet I couldn't bear to
watch them for a second longer. For the better part of that
year, Lucky had taken me out swimming every morning
without fail. I'd had my own legs wrapped around his waist
as he submerged my lower body into the water. Then he'd
gently unfurl my contracted limbs and guide my body across
the pool in his arms, as I floated on my back. He'd shown me
that it was possible for someone with a body like mine to defy
gravity, at a time in my life when I was starting to feel bogged
down by the weight of ableism.

There comes a point in virtually every disabled adult's life
when we are told, in no uncertain terms, to start living real-
istically, which is a coded way of saying that we should make
peace with not being able to do the things with our bodies
and our lives that nondisabled uprights get to do with theirs
all the time. The memo we get from our families, our communities, society at large, is as clear as can be: if you want to be
loved and cared for, reduce the size of your life and abide only
by that which is reasonable for someone outside of your experience to provide. Lucky, by enabling me to do things with

27

my life like go swimming, go out clubbing, go speed racing, had inspired me to be unreasonable in the way I'd desired to live. He'd say, "It's your fucking life. You wanna live slightly dangerously? Do it. You wanna swim? Swim."

In the process of learning to satisfy my craving for a larger, slightly dangerous life, I'd found myself developing a larger, slightly dangerous craving for Lucky. We'd have clandestine meetings where he'd often giggle flirtatiously and would even position himself really close to me, as if he meant to kiss me, before changing his mind at the very last second. In an ableist world, there were so few avenues for me to actualize romantic connection, and I was primed to believe any sort of attention, no matter how ambiguous, could potentially bloom into true love. But in the very same breath he was adamant that he could never, ever, be intimate with another man. "Never in a million years," he'd say in passing over lunch or after accompanying me on a date, which I respected. Now, as I watched in astonishment Lucky being intimate with a man, I immediately deduced that "never in a million years" had actually meant never in a million years with me.

But sitting there with my mouth hanging open, I found myself feeling more betrayed than rejected. *So much for being straight as they come,* I thought. It wasn't as though I didn't know that sexuality was fluid and complex. I'd taken doctoral-level courses in sexology and queer theory years ago as a sophomore in undergrad. My professors insisted that I was too bright for the introductory material, so they'd let me sneak into the

graduate classes in my spare time. Given my academic train-
ing, coupled with common sense, of course, I believed that
as a human being Lucky was perfectly entitled to move in
and out of various categories of desire as he pleased. In other
words, Lucky's sexuality was none of my goddamn business.
But in choosing to stick his tongue down my friend's throat
without regard for my presence, much less my feelings, he'd
just made it my business. It was not just inappropriate. It was
downright cruel. As far as I was concerned, this entire scene
had the makings of a hit-and-run. Lucky had just knocked me
down and then flattened me as he revved backward and sped
off with Maxwell in the passenger seat.

THREE

THE LAST TIME MY HEART had been broken was in undergrad, during my freshman year. He went by the name of KG, and he was also the first person I ever came out to. KG was a perfect all-rounder. He played on the basketball team, was an engineering major, and was always the most affable person in the room. As if he wasn't perfect enough, he also had the body of a god. On reflection, I think I liked KG because he was the first self-identified gay Black man I knew; I conflated seeing myself *in* him with seeing myself *with* him. I was drawn to how unbothered, how unburdened he was in the way he moved through the world. Sometimes he'd wear sweats with oversized headphones, projecting a cool, steely disposition. Other times he looked a bit like Steve Urkel from the American sitcom *Family Matters*, with his suspenders and tortoiseshell frames, playful and dorky. He was comfortable being who he was, and I liked that about him. He spoke about his sexuality with such ease that it gave me permission to step into—or, in this case, wheel into—my truth.

One evening, after we had dinner together in the school's cafeteria, we went for a stroll. In the days prior I'd gone back and forth with myself on whether I should just bite the bullet and come out to him. But every time I wanted to, the words themselves refused to come out. This time though, I was ready. "I'm gay," I told him, my insides bunched up in nerves.

"Sweet!" he said, without missing a beat. "Welcome to the club." Something about his swagger instantly disarmed me and made me even more intrigued by him. As time went on, our after-dinner strolls became a regular occasion. It didn't take long before he would show up at my door in the wee hours of the morning to talk. Just talk. We'd talk for hours on end. I would oblige, giddy with delight for the pleasure of his company. Slowly, surely, the subject of our conversations turned to his pursuit of a boy. A White boy. An athlete, like him. He told me he had a "preference" for what I already knew were generic, mediocre boys who like mayonnaise and who conflate jumping with dancing. To him, I was good enough to have six-hour-long conversations with and maybe cuddle with at three o'clock in the morning but not to actually date.

I thought he would grow to like me. So I continued to see him at ungodly hours and give him advice on how to snag the guy of his dreams, which, in due course, I hoped would turn out to be me. He was the only anchor I had to the burgeoning version of myself that was bubbling up inside of me. The risk of losing that connection was greater than the pain of being constantly sidelined. Then one evening, KG showed up at my door for a different reason. "I can't do this with you anymore," he muttered. We both knew that the time had come for us to confront the truth head-on: he had been shamelessly leading me on, and I was a willing participant.

I hyperventilated as I begged him to stay. Then I tried to tell him that I didn't care, that he could lead me on for as long as he wished. I tried to negotiate an arrangement. He saw the wild irrationality in my eyes. I suspect he felt deeply sorry for me—so much so that he wrapped his arms around me. I soaked his sleeves in my tears, crying nonstop for what must have been half an hour until he tried to say goodbye once and for all. But I refused to let him walk out of the front door. Not wanting to let him go but unable to use my arms, I used my teeth to cling to his bomber jacket. He yanked his arm away, releasing himself from my yearning, pleading mouth. I sobbed from the depths of my being as I watched him disappear out of the doorframe, out of my dorm room, and out of my life.

The next week, I dyed my Afro purple. I'd been so willing to have been made a fool of by a boy who demonstrated so little regard for me that I needed to reclaim that part of myself. I dyed my hair to prove to myself that I was in control of my life. After that, I came out as gay to everyone who crossed my path—students, faculty, and friends alike. I felt transcendent. That's when I realized: I didn't want to be unbothered and unburdened, like KG was—I wanted to be unapologetic and unorthodox. I was starting to like the way I moved, the way I breathed. I no longer needed to like KG in order to like myself.

But despite my spiritual growth after KG, I still found myself pining for the same profile of guy—brimming with charisma but totally emotionally unavailable. The only difference now was that Lucky was also my care aide. In some ways my current predicament was more heartbreaking. Because Lucky and I were with each other around the clock, there was no real way for me to bypass my feelings for him.

When Adrian returned with our drinks clasped between his hands, he noticed the gutted expression etched on my face. "What's wrong?" he asked, leaning in to speak directly into my ear.

"Take me home," I said. He still looked a beat behind, so I spoke up even louder, competing with the dancehall beats blaring in the background. "Adrian, take me home now." As he bent over to lay the drinks on a stool, he glanced up at the adjacent wall and saw what I regretted I'd seen. Adrian shook his head. He turned my chair on for me and escorted me back out through the hordes of uprights on the dance floor.

Emerging from what felt like a cave into the vast, interminable night, I wheeled myself around the corner, inhaled the crisp, cold air, and exhaled my broken heart. Adrian charged after me and held me in his arms. "It's okay. You're okay," he whispered, as he caressed the top of my head. Police sirens blaring in the background and the cackles of inebriated partygoers staggering past us punctuated my wailing as Adrian continued to hold my face against his chest. "I don't think you should take Lucky with you to Oxford."

My eyes widened.

"Eddie, he's messing with your head. He doesn't know what he wants."

I wiggled myself out of his embrace, straightening my posture. "I'll find a way," I said, sniffling. "I'll find a way to . . . to, I don't know, suppress my feelings or something, but there's no way in hell I'm losing Lucky as my care aide. No way. He's coming with me to Oxford."

Adrian cupped his hands over his face and started pacing around. "Eddie, listen to me," he said, stopping to part his hands until only his fingertips touched. "I get it, okay? Lucky is a stellar care aide. He's attentive and goes beyond the call of duty, but I can't allow you to sacrifice yourself for him," he added. "Here's the thing: the guy is a clinical fuckboy who knows you have feelings for him and is exploiting that knowledge for his own gain."

"You don't know what you're talking about," I snapped.

"Sheesh, Eddie, it's as clear as day. I wish you could see it for what it is, my brother. You bend over backward trying to keep him happy, hoping that he'll love you in return, and the little piece of shit is happy to keep stringing you along. It's the reason why your mom didn't show up tonight, isn't it? Because I can tell you now that we both see right through him."

I bit my lip to stop it from quivering. The truth of what Adrian had just said hurt. Perhaps more so than seeing Lucky and Maxwell locking lips back in the club. I knew that the dynamic between Lucky and me was off. That he had been in it for self-preservation all this time. But two things can be true at once. It was true that Lucky had been stringing me along. It was also true that neither Adrian nor Mom, who also shared a dislike for Lucky for the same set of reasons, fully appreciated that despite Lucky's shortcomings he was also precisely the sort of care aide I needed to be able to thrive. I was genuinely caught between a rock and a hard place. "What do you expect me to do? Lucky and I leave next week. Tomorrow we're supposed to get our visas. You, what? Want me to magically start walking between now and then?" I quipped in defense of my decision-making capabilities. "I don't know what you want me to do in this situation."

"What if...?" Adrian pondered. "What if your mom goes with you?"

I almost scoffed but restrained myself when I saw the earnestness in the arch of his brow. "My mom is a sixty-something-year-old woman with a bad back. You can't expect her to move halfway across the world and ask her to break her back further by caring for me full time," I said. "Besides, my mom has done her bit. She's brought me this far; the rest is now up to me." I loved my mother deeply. I became the person

I was because Mom had always been the woman she was: an indisputable force of nature. I knew Adrian meant well. But it angered me that he thought this was an acceptable suggestion. I was no different from him. I too wanted the opportunity to leave the nest, as it were, and explore the world as an autonomous adult, or as autonomously as the reality of my disabled lived experience would allow.

Adrian went quiet, letting the night sounds take over—honking cars, barking dogs, thudding footsteps, whirring engines, and shrill cries. "Yeah, I get it," he said eventually. "It just sucks seeing you hurt like this." The tears flowed unrelentingly, cascading down my cheeks as I fixed my gaze upon a distant streetlamp, its flickering light casting a haunting glow. "Come here," Adrian said, pulling me into a hug. "We'll figure it out together."

FOUR

LUCKY GENTLY POSITIONED ME against the plush con-
tinental pillows and arranged my limbs in a peaceful lotus
pose. After the tumultuous night, the crew had retired to
Thandie's penthouse to crash. There was an air of embarrassment between Lucky and me now, as we both knew that what
had occurred the previous night marked a significant turning
point in our relationship. However, neither of us was willing
to bring it up, and we carried on in uncomfortable silence.
Although I still relied on Lucky's help with my daily routines,
I was tempted to ignore him as a form of retribution for what
had happened at the club. But I couldn't dwell on this for
long. I needed to focus on more pressing matters: finalizing
my preparations for my upcoming life as an Oxford graduate
student.

"Lucky, could you fetch my laptop?" I asked before he ventured off to the bathroom to tend to himself. As he staggered away, I took a deep breath and mentally fortified myself. *I will be fine.* With my one good finger, I navigated to my Gmail account and was met with a barrage of emails, the most critical of which informed me that my visa had been approved but Lucky's had not. In a surprising turn of events, there was apparently no visa provision for a designated care aide accompanying an international student with a disability, a loophole neither the university nor the UK's Home Office had detected prior to this point.

I was struck with disbelief as I read the email correspondence before me. The only recourse available to me was to reach out to the list of local care agencies provided in the email in search of alternative arrangements.

I gazed at the email, my thoughts outpacing my ability to process them. The words before me seemed to blur and fade, and I struggled to comprehend the reality they conveyed. Hurt as I was, I couldn't imagine doing this without Lucky.

As I sat there, I was torn between two desires: the prestige of studying at Oxford, a bastion of knowledge and opportunity, and the deepening of my relationship with Lucky, who had been a constant support and source of comfort in my life.

On the one hand, despite everything, Lucky had always been there for me in the way that I needed him to be, validating my need to live unencumbered. On the other hand, Oxford represented a once-in-a-lifetime opportunity, a coveted prize that would demonstrate to the world that disability and achievement are not mutually exclusive. But why should I have to choose between my quality of life and the opportunity to build a legacy? It seemed like a cruel trade-off, like being asked to pick between two halves of my heart.

I took a deep breath, inhaling the courage I needed to face this decision. If I was being honest with myself, I was banking on the idea that if Lucky joined me in Oxford, maybe there'd be a chance for me to experience romantic love, yet another one of those things society would deem as incompatible with disability. But I suppose Adrian was right: the ambitions I held for myself and for the world ultimately needed to come first, like a compass pointing the way forward.

"I can do this," I whispered to myself. "I will find a way."

And so, right then and there, I made the difficult yet necessary decision to embark on my journey solo, without Lucky by my side. Though the path ahead might prove to be a tumultuous one, I could not allow my feelings for Lucky to impede my pursuit of my dreams.

Just as I came to this realization, Adrian appeared in the doorway, savoring an apple, his presence jolting me out of my ruminations. "What's up?" he asked with a crunch. "You're still upset 'bout last night?"

"I've changed my mind. I won't be going to Oxford with

Lucky," I proclaimed. Adrian's eyes widened in shock as he quickly closed the door and shuffled his way over, joining me on the bed.

"It's not about what you said last night," I reassured him as he spun my laptop around to read the email.

A lengthy silence filled the room before Adrian commented, "This is a big step, Eddie. It's time to break the rearview mirror and move forward."

His words resonated, seeping through me like a leaky pen would through a legal pad, reminding me of the speeches I had given around the world, encouraging disabled youth to give ableism the middle finger and not think twice. "I just need to get to Oxford. The rest will take care of itself," I declared with newfound resolve.

"Yes, yes, yes," Adrian cheered with a grin that stretched across his face. I knew he'd be overjoyed. "You're now part of an elite network. You needn't worry. Everything's going to get easier from here on out, for sure."

I nodded slowly, still trying to convince myself that, yes, indeed, everything was going to work out for me. "There's just one problem," I said. "How am I going to break the news to Lucky?"

Adrian pouted and squinted his eyes. "Leave that to me," he said. "I'll position your phone on your lap for you right now so you can cold-call the list of agencies they sent you. While you do that, I'll go with Lucky on a long-ass walk and break the news to him," he said, chuckling before turning serious again. "He'll understand. Trust me."

"WE ARE UNABLE TO FLY a care aide to Johannesburg," was the universal response I received as I reached out to various care agencies. My heart sank as I was faced with the same response a sixth time. "We can offer our services within the confines of the United Kingdom, but we are unable to fly a care aide to Johannesburg." Navigating the complex terrain of geopolitics and care was the reality of being a disabled international student, a hurdle I'd leapt to attend undergrad at Carleton University in Ottawa, Ontario, but with a fraction of this difficulty.

As I lay on my bed, feeling defeated and exhausted, a voice within me urged me to keep searching. I scoured the internet for care agencies in London that offered traveling nurses or care aides. It was on the third search result that I found an agency that stood out from the rest. I dialed the number with a glimmer of hope and was pleasantly surprised to hear a professional voice answer on the third ring.

The representative informed me that they had never served someone as young as twenty-six, but they saw the opportunity to add an Oxford graduate to their list of clients as a valuable business opportunity. Unlike the other agencies I had called, this one was not intimidated by the logistics of sending an aide to Johannesburg. It was a win-win situation.

As I brought the call to a close, I made one final request: "Could I ask that you please assign me a care aide who is strong, preferably a guy, as the nature of my disability is such that I need to be physically transferred several times throughout the day?" I pinched my face, bracing myself for the possibility that they might quibble their way out of such a request.

"That shouldn't be a problem, Eddie. I have someone in mind who'd be perfect," the representative said, to my relief. Thank heavens for #OxfordEddiecated. I was now able to use some of the £22,000 I'd raised as a down payment on a month's worth of care. "Let's deal with this one step at a time. We can worry about the details of your care plan for the rest of your studies once you're in the UK," the representative of the agency said. I gave them my card details, and that was that. When I hung up, I felt like I'd slid into a train seconds before it was about to bolt out of the station. I'd cried a lot already, but my ducts were clearly still full. *You're one step closer to Oxford. Hang in there, Eddie,* I thought.

Adrian and Lucky had not yet returned from their walk. I couldn't help but worry about the kind of conversation they were having and if Adrian was actually softening the blow or, yielding to schadenfreude, had opted to stick it to him instead. I guess I'd find out soon. In the meantime, I found myself feeling a pull in my heart and decided to call Mom to update her on the events of my life, or at least the parts that I felt comfortable sharing.

Mom was not only my mother but also my first care aide

and the last person I would ever want to disappoint or burden with my problems. Maybe I'd taken my desire for self-sufficiency too far, but I had always been cautious about revealing my struggles, only doing so once I had found a solution. I fully believed I had the spiritual endurance to get myself through my struggles so convincingly that no upright person or upright system could ever deny me my worth, not even my mom.

"I am so glad, Junior, you aren't taking that boy with you anymore. He's no good. My ancestors answered my prayers. The way you left home still breaks my heart, you know," Mom said. Earlier that year, I'd told Mom during a heated exchange that I could no longer live under the same roof as her after she'd scolded me for returning home from a club with Lucky at three o'clock in the morning. I was so enraged by what I'd believed was Mom's capstone attempt to strip me of my agency that I'd decided to wheel out the door with Lucky and check us into a cheap hotel downtown.

"I know, Moms, and I'm sorry. I just needed to live on my own terms as an adult. I needed to claim my agency," I said. Mom and I had been caught in the tension between protection and freedom, a complex dynamic shared by so many disabled adults and their parents or guardians. Mom had made me the center of her universe and, because of my vulnerability to unfair treatment, felt it her moral duty to protect me from the world. My self-actualization was my promise to myself, and I felt it my moral duty to move through the world fulfilling that

45

promise. We'd found ourselves in a situation where our individual convictions had bumped up against each other like fish in the sea, accidentally knocking each other to avoid crashing into anthropogenic pollutants, fuckboys, and ableism, to name a few.

Mom spoke with conviction in her voice, expressing her fears for me. "I hope you can see what happened through my eyes," she said. "I cannot simply stand by as my son's life is ruined."

The door slowly creaked open, and I could see Lucky and Adrian peeking in. Anxious anticipation washed over me. "Okay, Moms, I have to go now. I'll call you later. Love you."

"Okay, I love you," she replied with a touch of warmth in her voice.

As Lucky approached me, I could feel the hairs on my arms stand on end. I was nervous, hoping that everything had gone according to plan. He kindly removed my earphones and gave me a warm and comforting embrace. I rested my chin on his shoulder and caught a glimpse of Adrian giving me a reassuring thumbs-up from the doorway.

"I'll come visit," Lucky said, as he held me close. Closing my eyes, I felt a mixture of fear and uncertainty in my stomach. I knew our time together was coming to an end.

FIVE

As LUCKY AND I APPROACHED the underground parking lot at O.R. Tambo International Airport, I couldn't help but admire the sleek, modern design of the building. Its gleaming glass exterior seemed to reflect the bustling activity of the airport, with planes taking off and landing in the distance. The structure rose tall and proud into the sky, its sharp lines and angles giving it a sense of strength and stability. The entrance to the parking lot was marked by two imposing concrete columns, and as we approached, I could see that the floor was made of smooth, polished marble. Overall, the building exuded a sense of efficiency, power, and sophistication. The sound of the engine of our vehicle echoed through the concrete walls of the garage, adding to the tension building within me. The fluorescent lights overhead flickered and buzzed, casting an eerie glow on the empty spaces around us.

Lucky slowed the car down as we approached the ticket booth and the parking attendant. I held my breath, my eyes fixed on Lucky's outstretched hand as he reached for the parking slip. The anticipation was palpable as he brushed against the slip with his fingers, about to grasp it.

Just then, my phone rang, disrupting the stillness of the moment. I answered the call, trying to keep my voice steady, but I could feel my heart racing. The sound of the traffic outside and the music from my earbuds blended, creating a cacophony that only added to the tension in the air.

"Hello?" I answered, my voice tinged with curiosity.

"Hey, Eddie," a jarring Welsh accent greeted me on the other end of the line. "My flight landed ahead of schedule. You'll find me waiting on one of the benches at arrivals. Take your time, though. Just wanted to give you a heads-up." It was my new care aide, whom I was meant to meet at the airport. We had made arrangements with the agency for her to arrive several hours earlier so that she could spend the day with Lucky and me, getting to know the ropes of my care before our departure.

I was initially informed that my care aide was a man, but I'd received a surprise call from the agency the night before, informing me of a last-minute change. "Good evening, Eddie. Sorry to bother. I hope you're looking forward to your flight out tomorrow. The male care aide we'd identified for you has unfortunately had to return to Iran for a family emergency," the representative had said. "But don't worry, our traveling nurse will fetch you. She's wonderful. She's also incredibly strong, so you'll be in good hands."

Though the sudden change in care aide was unexpected, I was just grateful that the agreement I'd made with the agency was still in place. I was eager to get the process started and leave any potential roadblocks behind.

"Hey! Great to hear from you. Hope you traveled well. Listen, we're actually already here. Just looking for a spot to park," I said.

"Great. Looking forward to meeting you," she said, her voice croaky with a tinge of nervousness.

I hung up the phone and watched through the side-view mirror of the car as the red-and-white beam behind us fell, as if it were a guillotine, slicing my present from what already felt like my past. Lucky pulled into a wheelchair-accessible parking spot near the terminal entrance and cut the engine.

As he removed his hands from the steering wheel, I couldn't bring myself to look at him. I didn't want to risk expressing my feelings, saying something like "I'll miss you" or "How could you?" or even something reckless and impulsive like "Kiss me." I had to remain focused on what lay ahead and accept that there was no turning back.

We scoured the expansive, amphitheater-like hall, searching with our inquiring eyes for a welcoming face. As we made our way through the neat rows of plastic chairs, which were securely fastened to the floor, and wound through the rotunda, I caught a glimpse of a woman striding back and forth in front of the currency exchange counter. Her hand was buried deep in the pocket of her form-fitting jeans, and a single, camouflaged backpack was slung over her shoulder. This was unmistakably the person we were searching for. It was clear from her limited possessions that this was just a quick drop-off and pickup mission.

As she turned, our eyes met, and I couldn't help but be struck by her appearance. Her tousled strawberry-blonde hair was a stark contrast to her pale, round face and framed it perfectly. She wore a practical khaki trench coat that was draped over her blue jeans and sturdy work boots. She looked as if she had stepped straight out of the pages of one of those study-abroad brochures that promise adventure to the bright-eyed, adventurous college students of the Northern Hemisphere who are eager to experience the challenges of a little-known African city.

She gave a small wave and I wheeled myself closer to her, taking in her warm, inviting eyes and a smile that was full of life and character. As I reached her, I couldn't help but feel enveloped in a sense of trust and comfort emanating from her very presence. She seemed like a calming force in the midst of the chaos and noise of the bustling hall.

We introduced ourselves to one another. She was the first of many care aides I would encounter in the coming year, and I would soon come to refer to her as "One" in my mind.

"This is Lucky, by the way, the person whose huge shoes you're here to fill," I jokingly said.

"Nice to, meet you, Lucky," One replied with a smile as they shook hands in the airport terminal. "Shall we?"

As we stepped out of the terminal, One became a veritable chatterbox. She regaled us with an entertaining story about her layover flight to Addis Ababa, where she sat next to a woman who had evaded airport security and smuggled food that ended up causing a stink in the cabin.

Along the way, we made a stop to feed the parking ticket into the machine. Even though we were only gone for a short time, we still had to pay for the time we spent at the airport. While Lucky took care of that, One launched into another captivating story about her experience working for a sheikh who offered to buy her a Rolls Royce, but she turned it down because she believed in being of service to others in need.

On the walk back to the car park, One's conversation bounced between her boyfriend, an engineer, and her ninety-year-old great grandmother, both of whom she loved deeply. The chatter finally subsided when Lucky opened the door of the passenger seat and began transferring me out of my wheelchair.

"This is the proper way to lift someone," Lucky said, as he held me firmly in his arms, with my head resting against his chest. "Lift with your legs apart, using your quads, biceps, and pecs. Never lift with your lower back or you'll hurt yourself," he warned before fastening my seat belt.

Once at Thandie's place, Lucky showed One the ins and outs of feeding me, how to properly position my hand on my chair's joystick, and what to keep in mind when monitoring me overnight. Properly briefed and surrounded by the comforting familiarities of home, One shared her experiences as a care aide with me.

"I've been doing this for a few years now, and I've never seen someone treat their client with the kind of care and attention that Lucky shows you," she said. "Most aides treat their clients like just a number, but Lucky treats you like a person."

One's words caught me off guard. I had always appreciated Lucky's care, but I had never thought about how he might be different from other aides.

One must have noticed my surprise because she quickly added, "I apologize if I spoke out of turn. I just wanted to let you know that I noticed the difference and I think it's wonderful. I promise to do my best to be the same with you."

BEFORE DESCENDING INTO THE SECURITY checkpoint and passport control, I swiveled my chair to catch one more glimpse of Adrian, Thandie, and Lucky. As they waved goodbye from the check-in counters, I gazed back at them and felt a wave of sadness wash over me. The tears flowed freely down my cheeks as I turned away from my friends and the lover I'd never have. One tried to offer comfort, but I was lost in my thoughts and unable to take solace in her words. This journey marked the end of an era, a departure from the ones who had stood by my side through thick and thin.

The sound of my wheelchair rolling down the jet bridge heightened my feelings of anticipation. The rickety structure trembled beneath me as I made my way toward the airplane door. The flight attendants, who were checking boarding passes, turned their attention to me, their expressions shifting from warm smiles to awkward grimaces. The protocol dictated that I should have boarded the plane first, but someone had failed to follow protocol. They scrambled to make way for me, but even the yellow-jacketed support staff seemed uncertain. They stood agape, unsure of what to do next. The moment was marked by confusion and hesitation, a poignant reminder of the challenges that lay ahead.

Then one of the flight attendants, the most prim of the lot, with a fashion model's figure, wheeled out a slipper chair from behind a storage area, used for transferring immobile passengers on and off the aircraft. On closer inspection, the slipper chair looked like a straitjacket folded upright. As the flight attendant clasped the uppermost part of its long backrest, I couldn't help but notice her French manicure. *Those hands don't look like they've lifted anything heavier than thirty pounds,* I thought. "How do we do this?" she asked.

I felt like an undesirable object nobody wanted to touch. "I've got it," One chirped, slicing through the thick layer of awkwardness that hung in the air like billowing smoke. She squatted, parting her legs. Then she tucked one hand inside my armpit and the other behind the bend of my knees and, with one clean swoop, transferred me from my wheelchair to the slipper chair, exactly as Lucky had shown her.

"For someone who's never done this before, you're really good. That was perfect," I said, feeling equal parts impressed and relieved as I was being strapped into the slipper chair. The flight attendant took over for the easy part, wheeling me down the aisles and toward my seat in the business class cabin. When we reached my row, she stood back and motioned for One to salvage the situation once more. One scooped me up, just as effortlessly as before, and gently plonked me into my seat.

As soon as One got me comfortable, I gave Mom a quick call before takeoff to channel my excitement and apprehension for what lay ahead. "Bon voyage, my son," she said, her voice filled with pride. "You've always been brave. You took over ALA, and you will conquer Oxford. Spread your wings and fly." And with those words ringing in my ears, I closed my eyes and braced myself for what I hoped would be the adventure of a lifetime.

She was right. I'd done this before. Just shy of my sixteenth birthday, Mom returned from the grocery store with a stack of magazines. Mom devoured the glossy pages stamped with the latest articles and write-ups on the politics of post-Apartheid South Africa. As I sat on the couch and paged through one of them, my condition less developed at the time, I came across a double-page spread of a feature about the newly created African Leadership Academy, ALA for short, an A-Level boarding school on the outskirts of Johannesburg for gifted young people between sixteen and eighteen with the potential to transform the continent…and the world. The more I read, the larger my eyes grew. The feature concluded with a call for applications from the academy's founders: "We are looking for the brightest minds to join the inaugural class."

My entire being said, *This is it.*

Several weeks later, I was trying to convince Mom to allow me to fly to Johannesburg for the finalists' weekend. No parents were allowed, and that meant no one to look after me. But the academy assured her that I would be in good hands, so she reluctantly agreed. It was the first and only time I'd fly unaided.

Chris, one of the cofounders of the academy, graciously offered to step in as my care aide for the entire duration of the weekend trip. As he carried me into the bathtub Saturday morning of finalists' weekend, I felt his hands tremble under the weight of my body. He had clearly never done this before. I wondered whether he knew just how much courage it required from me to hold space for both of us. The moment demanded that I rise above the terrifying awkwardness I felt being bathed by this white American man, whom I did not know from the bar of soap he was holding, so that he wouldn't feel paralyzed by his nerves.

As Chris lathered me up with soap, I refused to allow

silence to take root. I spoke his ear off. Like an actor auditioning for their dream role, I pretended to be relaxed and unfazed. Once he caught on and relaxed as well, I, in turn, started to feel calm and at ease. While he splashed water over me in the most pitifully tentative of ways, I pushed through my fear and told him that I was ready to assume my spot in the inaugural class, come what may. I had to prove that there was no contradiction—none whatsoever—between embodying the stuff future world leaders are made of and moving through the world as a physically disabled person. It was the most important interview, over and above the official one, that I knew I had to ace.

At the end of the weekend, as Chris bade me farewell at the airport and handed me over to a flight attendant, he crouched down in the middle of the check-in line, put his hand on my shoulder, and spoke to me with a frog in his throat: "You are one of a kind, Eddie." Chris's words rang in my ears and made me feel invincible and hopeful about the future.

It was now Mom's words ringing in my ears and giving me hope about the future. We'd been down this road before. Just as she'd done all those years ago, she was being asked once again to lean into faith and let me go in support of my dreams.

"I love you, Mom," I said, hanging up just as one of the flight attendants offered me a choice between water and champagne before takeoff.

"Water, please," I replied.

One, slouching in the seat next to me, chimed in and said,

Sipping Dom Pérignon Through a Straw

"No bubbly to toast your next chapter?" I wasn't feeling particularly celebratory. In fact, I struggled to place the feeling. It was like a mixture of grief and anticipation. I was finally on my way to Oxford, institutional barriers be damned. Simultaneously, I was already missing the life and the people I was leaving behind, especially Lucky. "Nah," I said. "Perhaps when we get to Oxford. I think I'm going to skip dinner too. I'd like to recline all the way down and sleep as soon as we're airborne." One nodded. I could tell that she'd noticed the bittersweet tears in my eyes, but she was gracious enough to pretend as though she hadn't. "Of course, you've had a long day. Tell me what to do and I'll gladly put you to bed."

SIX

ONE AND I MADE OUR descent toward London's Heathrow International Airport. As I peered from my aisle seat out through the windows perforating the sides of the aircraft's body, the sky seemed to have split open, allowing the first rays of dawn to penetrate the clouds and bathe the business class cabin in warm light. I basked in the sun's embrace, sore from the long flight but filled with hope and the promise of a new beginning. The thought that I was about to land not only in London but on the soil of self-actualization brought a sense of excitement and purpose. This journey, I knew, would be the fruition of my labors, the place where I would cultivate a life abundant and rich. Oxford, I believed, would be the place where I could harvest the rewards of all my hard work.

"Ladies and gentlemen, welcome to Heathrow's Terminal 5.

Local time is 6:45 a.m. and the temperature is a glorious thirteen degrees Celsius. For your safety and comfort, please remain seated with your seat belt fastened until the captain turns off the Fasten Seat Belt sign. If you require deplaning assistance, please remain in your seat until all other passengers have deplaned. One of our crew members will then be pleased to assist you..."

I turned to One and with googly eyes whispered, "That's us!"

"...On behalf of British Airways and the entire crew, I'd like to thank you for flying with us. We look forward to seeing you on board again in the near future. Wishing you a pleasant onward journey."

Long after everyone else had disembarked I slouched back in my pod, waiting and waiting and waiting for my wheelchair to be retrieved from the belly of the plane. I feared that when I'd eventually be taken to the aircraft door, I'd look on in horror to find a swarm of burly uprights in yellow vests with inscrutable faces towering over what yesterday was my wheelchair but what was now a heap of dismembered aluminum parts. It's risky business flying while disabled. There's an assumption that our devices are nice-to-have equipment rather than essential mobility aids. What's often lost in the conversation about airline staff failing to handle our devices with care is that damage done to a wheelchair, for example, is actually an injury inflicted on the disabled person for whom that chair is their only mode of movement. While God-knows-what was unfolding on the tarmac, the flight attendants who'd been tasked to wait with One and me tried to assuage my anxiety by offering us water. I didn't want water. I didn't want tea. I didn't want another complimentary set of business class pajamas. I just wanted my chair and to be able to disembark the plane with dignity like everyone else had already done. "It's here," I finally heard someone say.

When my chair greeted me at the aircraft door in one piece, I closed my eyes and thanked my lucky stars in recognition of how rare an outcome such as this one was for those of us with the temerity to travel while disabled. Feeling relieved, One and I forged ahead, making our way through passport control and beyond the bright yellow sliding doors emblazoned with the word *EXIT*. We then hopped onto the Heathrow Express train bound for Paddington Station. From there we still had to take another train bound for Oxford itself.

We pulled into Paddington Station and I found myself craning my neck out the window in amazement to appreciate the architectural wonder of the train station. The single, enclosed structure felt like an entire city in its own right. As the belly of the train rumbled over the tracks, One sat forward, adopted an official posture, and said, "Right, my dear, this is where our journey together ends." I cocked my head to the side and arched an eyebrow. This was not the plan. "I'll be handing you over to one of our nicest and most experienced care aides," she said. "You guys would get along beautifully. She's also from Africa, you know?" *And you'd get along beautifully with my mom's best friend, Valentina, she's also from Europe, you know?* I thought sarcastically. I stared at her blankly, letting the well-meaning but problematic nature of the remark slide. I found it strange that I was only being informed of this now, but ensuring that my weary body actually got to Oxford felt more important than getting into it with One at the train station, of all places.

"We believe she's best suited to meet your needs as you begin your new chapter at Oxford," One continued. Then, after surveying the train car for eavesdroppers, she leaned in and said tentatively, "One more thing. We're not entirely sure she'll be able to physically lift you. You should know that health and safety regulations here in the UK forbid us as home care professionals from lifting clients, but don't you worry your precious little cheeks—I'm sure we can figure something out." I wondered what the point was of having Lucky show her the ropes only for her to abandon me before my real journey had even started. But exhausted and desperate, I nodded half-smilingly, with the acceptance at the back of my mind that starting a new life in a new country meant rolling with the punches.

The train came to a complete stop. As I carefully wheeled myself over the gap between the train and the platform, I looked up to find a sea of uprights glaring down at me, rustling with impatience. I caught myself smiling at them meekly: a coded apology for trespassing into their domain that I'd long abandoned but reflexively adopted in this unfamiliar territory. A few reluctantly gave way for me to pass, but the majority acted as if they hadn't seen me. It had been two years since I had last lived in a country with a wheelchair-accessible transit system, and I had to remind myself quickly that if I didn't start relearning how to give the uprights attitude when navigating my way through public spaces I would be trampled, both literally and figuratively. So I elongated my neck, pursed my lips, and pressed into the unresponsive crowd. If they accidentally got rammed, they'd have only their refusal to share space with a nonupright to blame. "Slow down!" One yelled, as she trailed behind me, dragging my jumbo-sized luggage in one hand and flinging her camouflage backpack over her shoulder with the other.

"Do you have a license for that thing?" One joked when she eventually caught up with me. Feeling cranky from the taxing journey, not to mention anxious about being handed off to someone new all over again, I wasn't in the mood for upright humor. But One was making an effort to be on my side, and I didn't want to be rude. I turned to her and said, "It's expired." She found this hysterical, so much so that she made us stop in our tracks so she could take a second to bend over, rest her hands above her knees, and laugh out loud. Only after she composed herself could she see from the grimace on my face that I wasn't quite as into it as she was.

"We have about twenty minutes to kill before your new care aide gets here," One said. "Anything you wanna do while we wait?" I scoped out my surroundings, and like sniper crosshairs, my eyes targeted the liquor store sandwiched in the corner. "Actually, I'd like to pick up that bottle of bubbly for later so I can toast my first night in Oxford."

"Lovely idea," she said.

We emerged from the liquor store with a bottle of cheap Prosecco. I couldn't help but smile when One discreetly tucked the sparkling wine away in my suitcase. I sat there wondering how I was going to continue feeding my appetite for the finer things in life as a cash-strapped student over the next year. As far as I was concerned, figuring out how to be bougie on a budget was going to be just as important as figuring out how to juggle a full course load while enjoying all that Oxford would have to offer.

We continued moving. Along the way, One stopped and pointed at an obscure kiosk selling Union Jack paraphernalia and what looked like bland coffee in short Styrofoam cups. "That's where we're supposed to meet your new care aide. It's time anyway, so let's walk over." When we got closer, a stubby-looking woman with black-and-lilac ombré box braids stood in the middle of the walkway, clasping the handle of a medium-sized neon-pink hard-shell suitcase while a blurry continuum of bodies whizzed past her. Of course, One hadn't mentioned where exactly on the African continent this woman was from, but as I briefly took inventory of her, I was able to infer from her unfazed posture that she, like me, was an Afropolitan—someone who'd successfully fended off one draconian visa regime after the next possibly to end up in

Sipping Dom Pérignon Through a Straw

Amsterdam tutoring one year, only to find oneself in Brazil two years later working for an environmental justice not-for-profit, all in pursuit of opportunity. "Over here," One called, waving her hand in the air.

We didn't have much time to exchange pleasantries, as the next train to Oxford was already boarding. One gestured to me, saying to the woman with the box braids, whom we henceforth shall refer to as "Two," "This is the famous Eddie." I bowed my head facetiously. "As you know, Eddie is also from Africa," One said as she began briefing Two. "He has Spinal Muscular Atrophy, so he requires around-the-clock support, but I can tell you that from the few hours I've spent with him he's quite possibly the sweetest guy you'll ever meet, and not to mention super smart, but, duh, that's obvious considering that he just got accepted into Oxford," One chortled. Two, on the other hand, grinned in amazement, as if she were dying to code switch so she could snap her fingers and say something like *Come through Black excellence.* "I'll let you guys get acquainted on the ride to Oxford, but before you guys go I need to quickly talk you through how to physically lift him whenever you need to transfer him in and out of his chair."

Two scrunched her face. "Lift him?"

"I know what you're thinking, but he prefers to be carried in and out of his wheelchair when going to the bathroom, traveling, et cetera, whatever the situation," One replied. If I could, I'd have given her a big fat hug for essentially saying, *Eff these rules that don't make no goddamn sense.* But I also would have probably made a slight correction to her comment. This wasn't a preference. In fact, her remark kind of confused me. How else was I supposed to be transferred? It was that or a hoist, which was simply impractical and frankly dehumanizing to transport and use.

"He's not that heavy. I carried him on and off the plane." One said, unfazed and hyperaware of the time. Two looked unconvinced. "Right, when getting ready to lift, stand with your legs apart, suck in your stomach, and lift using your calves, thighs, and biceps, never your lower back. Then lift, holding him as close to your body as possible, gently putting him down afterward," One explained while Two's mouth hung open. "Let me quickly demonstrate." Before I knew it, One scooped me up from my seat like a baby. I felt like a prop but went along with it. I knew I had to put my feelings of self-consciousness aside for the sake of the larger goal. This was the bumpy road to Oxford. "See," she yelped, unbothered by the glare of passersby. One immediately plopped me back into my seat and said, "You guys need to run, so I won't let you practice here."

I scanned Two's face for reassurance but couldn't find any. She was the same height as me, seated. My wheelchair height was five foot one. Had I been an upright, with no contractures in my knees, I'd have probably been about six foot two. Looking at Two, I noticed she carried quite a bit of flab around her waist. But I swiftly reprimanded myself for betraying my own body positivity politics and equating her weight and appearance with her level of strength. Maybe, hopefully, she would pull through. I fixed my face with a broad smile and said, "Between the two of us I'm sure we can figure it out."

"Right. Of course. We've got this," Two muttered, remembering to close her mouth and to also fix her face with a smile, though hers wasn't nearly as big as mine.

"Well, then, I think you guys are all set," One declared, shoving my luggage into Two's hands. "Such a pleasure, Eddie. Don't hesitate to call us if you need anything. Best of luck."

I'm going to need it, I thought.

SEVEN

Dᴜʀɪɴɢ ᴛʜᴇ ɴᴇᴀʀʟʏ ʜᴏᴜʀ-ʟᴏɴɢ ᴊᴏᴜʀɴᴇʏ from London's Paddington Station to Oxford, Two and I bonded over the initial discovery that we were, serendipitously, both proud exports of southern Africa, siblings of the same soil. I let her do most of the talking as I was too tired to even move my mouth. She told me a bit about her childhood growing up in Zimbabwe and then recounted her unlikely trajectory from Bulawayo to Reading, Berkshire, where she'd been living for the past twelve years.

When we arrived in Oxford, we hailed a wheelchair-accessible cab, an ostensibly mundane activity that still filled me with wonder despite the fact that I'd hailed many a cab on past occasions. In so many parts of the world, freedom of movement—on the ground and in the air—remained a fundamental right flagrantly denied to disabled people. You could never tell where it would be easy and where it would be impossible. "Where to?" our driver asked as soon as we successfully stuffed ourselves into the vehicle.

"Somerville College," I replied, wide-eyed like a child, from the back of the iconic British black cab. I peered out through the window, marveling at the way the sun bounced off of the cobblestone pavements, just as it did in the images and movies I'd seen of picturesque European cities like Prague, Venice, and Paris. It's funny how you can feel sentimental about a place you've never set foot in. The driver's eyes locked with mine in the rearview. "Wanna listen to some music?" he asked.

"Sure," I replied. Britney Spears spilled out from the radio and Y2K nostalgia took over as I found myself lip-syncing to every word, just as I'd done as a child. I was nine going on ten when I wanted nothing more in life than to be Britney Spears. In hindsight, it wasn't so much about wanting to be the American pop sensation herself but about wanting to embody the stuff of which stars like her were made. Britney was an unstoppable, undeniable force of creative genius for so many of us brought up on a daily diet of pop culture at the turn of the century. She was pop's high priestess.

The morning when the music video to her smash hit "Oops!...I Did It Again" premiered on Namibian television in the autumn of 2000, I woke up extra early, outpacing the sun so that I wouldn't miss a single second of the bubble-gum extravaganza. Wide awake, I rolled over onto my stomach and maneuvered myself until the length of my little frame was perfectly lined up against the long edge of my bed. Then I dropped my left leg to the bedroom floor like an anchor plummeting down to the ocean floor, using the weight to slide the rest of my body off the bed. Like a baby giraffe struggling to regain its balance, I dug my knees into the carpet, arched my back, and held myself up with my elbows, resting my chin— and by extension my lollipop head—between the palms of my hands. This was how I "walked" around the house as a disabled kid not yet tethered to my wheelchair. Walking with two legs was a rather banal and pedestrian way of sauntering through the world to me anyway, so I had invented a new mode of human movement. The planet's nondisabled ambulatory population, the uprights, simply did not know what they were missing.

On the verge of imploding with anticipation for Britney, I let out a squeal and then "walked" out of my room. Along the way, I passed the next room, where Mom was sound asleep. For a chronically exhausted single parent like herself, weekend sleep was sacred. I eventually made it into the main living area, where my younger brother, Wonga, was already plastered to the floor, remote control in hand. Wonga and I shared an abiding interest in pop culture, so naturally Britney was a central figure in our entertainment universe. First, we had to sit through KTV's weekend morning programming. It started with *Barney and Friends*, which we turned our noses up at. As far as we were concerned, that was a kiddie show. And at the ripe old ages of eight and nine and a half, respectively, we had graduated from kiddie television. *The Powerpuff Girls* and *Batman and Robin* followed immediately after, which were more up our alley. We sat through those cartoons like concertgoers impatient for the opening act to wrap up so that the headliner could take the stage. We wanted Britney above everything else.

The veejays eventually took over the airwaves, and with their classic boisterous introduction, the moment young people across the world had been waiting for all week finally arrived. The music video opened with a tilted shot of Britney in a glossy-red latex catsuit. It quickly transitioned to a wide shot of the pop princess breaking a sweat alongside a small army of backup dancers dressed in outfits that looked like tinfoil. The entire spectacle was set against the backdrop of an extraterrestrial landscape. For four minutes and twelve seconds, Wonga and I barely blinked. I could only think one thing: *this is who I want to be when I grow up.* Here was a young woman, bursting with ambition, who left her small town to pursue her dream of an extraordinary life on the world stage. She eventually succumbed to the viciousness of the tabloid industry, but not before she inspired young people like me, who were still in search of language to articulate our burgeoning queerness, to embrace ourselves in all our sassy, free-spirited glory. The seeds of my own dream of an extraordinary life on the world stage were sown that morning. Now, as we drove past one ancient building after the next, listening to Britney felt extra special—almost as if this was a personal dedication from her to me, providing the soundtrack for what I imagined was going to be my best era yet.

"You from out of town?" our driver asked.

"Yes, I am from South Africa. Johannesburg," I replied.

"Ah, Nelson Mandela."

It's been like twenty-two years since Mandela led the country to freedom. I can't believe he's still the only South African people can think of, but whatever, I thought.

"Yep," I said. He paused to flick the turn signal on the steering wheel as we rounded a bend.

"I am from Egypt." I looked back at him in the rearview and offered him a smile that I sincerely hoped would compensate for my lack of enthusiasm. Every muscle in my body was stiff. All I could think of was finding the nearest bed on which to lay my worn-out body so I could recharge in silence.

"Lovely," I said.

"You're in town just visiting?" he asked.

"No, sir. I just enrolled as a master's student at the university." Another pause, but this time to make way for the tear that ran down his face and found refuge in his coily salt-and-pepper beard. "*MashaAllah.* You must be Africa's Stephen Hawking," he said. "My sister's son is handicapped. He's thirteen years old. What you will go on to do when you graduate from this very prestigious university will one day change his life, *InshaAllah.*" He got me with that. I suddenly found myself becoming emotional. I knew that his nephew was probably not in school. He was the disabled kid denied access to mainstream education I'd been advocating for since I was sixteen years old. I fought back tears because I could see in my driver's eyes how he'd just drawn a straight line of possibility between his nephew's life and this moment dropping a young disabled African off on the grounds of the world's number one university.

It took me a moment to compose myself. "What's your nephew's name, sir?" I asked.

"Ahmed," he replied.

"I'm doing this for Ahmed," I said as we continued to lock eyes.

Moments later, he remembered Two was in the vehicle too. "What about you, my sister? You're also an Oxford student?"

"I wish," she said, as she giggled self-consciously. "No, I'm just his care aide."

Our driver slowed down as we approached Somerville College, which, to my delight, was the most charming of the Gothic buildings on its street. A line of cars snaked ahead of us. Students carrying luggage and boxes spilled out of each one and onto the sidewalk. You could spot the newbies from the oldies. The newbies, fresh to campus, shrieked, cackled, and skipped their way into the building. The oldies grimaced, yawned, and meandered their way across the threshold.

As we moved up in the queue, my mind began to wander to the peculiar organizational structure of Oxford. Unlike most universities, it operated as a federal system, much like the United States, where its 44 colleges, including Somerville, functioned with quasi-independence—akin to the 50 American states. This intricate configuration meant that earning a degree from Oxford was a three-part endeavor. An Oxonian would have to graduate from their specific department or school, their respective college, and, when combined, from the university itself.

Chuckling softly, I extended the analogy, wondering to myself which state Somerville was most going to resemble. Would it be a bastion of liberalism akin to the ever-progressive California? Or would it mirror the kaleidoscopic culture of New York? Or, perhaps, it would embody the natural splendor and jaw-dropping magnificence of Colorado? The possibilities were endless, and my mind was aflutter with fanciful musings.

I caught a glimpse of the entrance to the residential and academic community I was now a member of. Like the gilded frame of a Renaissance landscape portrait, the archway revealed a manicured courtyard, beyond which stood the hallowed grounds of the rest of the college. As soon as we were out of the taxi, our suitcases securely in Two's grasp, our driver circled his way around the body of the vehicle and waddled over to me. He tipped my face forward and gently kissed my forehead. "All the best, my brother," he said. As he climbed back into the idling car, he looked at Two and said, "Take good care of my friend. He's going to change the world."

When Two and I emerged on the other side of the archway, an official-looking woman was there to greet us. "You must be Eddie," she said. "I'm one of the college representatives. Welcome to your new home." I nodded and mouthed a thank-you. Two extended her arm for a handshake. "Hi, I'm Eddie's care aide."

"Delighted to make your acquaintance," the college representative responded, as she shook Two's hand. "You must be pooped, Eddie. Your room is still being renovated. Might be a few more weeks before it's ready, but in the meantime we have you staying in another room overlooking the lovely courtyard. Let me take you there now." *Strange,* I thought. *But I suppose it's only temporary. As long as I get to lay my head on a comfortable bed tonight, I'll worry about everything tomorrow.* We navigated between the rose beds that divided the courtyard into smaller quadrants. As I drove over the cobblestone pathways, the vibration from the uneven surface destabilized my control, flinging my hand off of the joystick. I stopped to tighten my grip.

"You're okay?" Two asked, compelling the college representative, who was leading the way, to stop in her tracks as well.

I hesitated. And immediately I thought back to the cobblestone streets of Italy during the first European trip I'd ever taken. A newly minted eighteen-year-old, I'd found myself in the fishing town of Bari, where I was one of nearly 1,500 changemakers attending the inaugural World Youth Summit.

Sipping Dom Pérignon Through a Straw

On the last day of that trip, the nurse who had accompanied me took me out for a stroll. Along the way, my wheels got stuck in the grooves of the rugged paving, and I was hurled out of my wheelchair and sent flying through the air. I was eventually stopped when my right eye made contact with the pavement, right in front of the Versace boutique. The bleeding was bad. When I returned to South Africa, I told everyone that the black eye was because I had "shopped until I dropped"— my lighthearted attempt at softening the blow of the news of what had happened. But now, flashback fresh in my mind, I wondered how I was going to soften the blow to these women ' that, no, I kinda wasn't fine. Was this what it was going to be like wheeling myself around? *I shouldn't complain on my first day here,* I thought. *Especially not about the quintessentially Oxford cobblestone. They're part of the charm of the place.* Perhaps my feelings were colored by the fact that I'd expended all my energy traveling. So I held my tongue, sort of. "Yeah," I whimpered. "I am okay. I am going to have to get used to the paving."

The college representative looked down at the ground. "Yes, the paving truly is magnificent, isn't it?" she said. "I too find myself having to stop to take it in."

Not what I meant, but sure. In truth, there was nothing romantic about unset paving. *This shit is treacherous,* I thought to myself as the joystick vibrated in my hands, making it that much more difficult to control my chair. Nevertheless, I forged ahead.

We stopped in front of the sort of building one imagines

would house the aristocratic characters in a Jane Austen novel. It was sophisticated, but in a way that wasn't vulgar. Actually, it was rather quaint. The entryway hid behind a cluster of trees whose leaves shimmied in the breeze. The college representative reached inside her pocket and pulled out a medieval set of keys held together by an oversized brass hoop. As she fiddled with the keys, searching for the right one to unlock the front door, she peeked over her shoulder and said, "Don't quote me on this, Eddie, but I suspect you'll be living in the very room Margaret Thatcher lived in when she studied here many moons ago. You're in eminent company." I stifled a laugh, knowing that I, a left-leaning, queer Black man from a former British colony, would be occupying a space the iconic conservative leader, who'd once been a staunch defender of the Apartheid regime, had previously inhabited. She'd have turned in her grave. *Only my ancestors could have orchestrated such cosmic justice,* I thought.

After unlocking the boulder of a door, the college representative forced it open with the bony part of her left shoulder. The door creaked open, and she stumbled into the hallway with it. She took a minute to readjust her posture with the self-consciousness of someone who'd just been put on the spot. "Follow me," she said, as she flicked her hair away from her face and swayed forward.

As she led us down a narrow hallway, I looked up at the ceiling and counted two, maybe even three, blown bulbs. Something about the mismatch between the building's charming exterior and its sterile, institutionalized interior unnerved me, as if it was foreshadowing something ominous. "Right, Eddie, this is you," the college representative said as she slowly pushed open a partially closed door that revealed what was, for all intents and purposes, a bare room. Beyond a stripped-down bed propped up against the wall in the corner and the rickety desk next to it, there was nothing else to take in but the grayscale stone walls. Not even the window above the desk that overlooked the courtyard was enough to brighten up the space. The only enticing thing in the small room was a curious package encased in Bubble Wrap sitting atop the desk. I curled my upper lip toward my nostrils as the waft of a hard-to-place odor traveled through the air. *If this is the cumulative BO of all the people who've ever lived here, then I bet my bottom dollar that Thatcher's the main culprit,* I quipped to myself.

The college representative trotted across the room as if she were a real estate agent showcasing a listing. "Lovely," she said, a word that felt terribly imprecise as a description for the space. "I am going to let you settle in and get some rest now, Eddie." Just before bolting for the door, she glanced over her shoulder in Two's direction and said, "Your room is right next door so you can be close to him in case he needs anything."

The college representative handed Two our copies of the key and shut the door behind her. I surveyed my surroundings and inhaled deeply. "I know we probably need to start unpacking, but I'm really curious about that parcel. Could you go ahead and unwrap it for me, please?" I asked.

"Of course, I'm curious about it myself," Two said. As she methodically unwrapped the package in question, I could make out what it was before the wrapping fully came off.

"Ah, excellent," I said. "My commode chair. I'm so glad Oxford procured it and had it shipped prior to my arrival. Now I can shower. Oh my God, I feel so yucky. It's been like thirty-six hours since I've bathed. So gross. I know we've just met, but I also—"

"Eddie, I, um...," Two said, cutting me off. "Look, I think there must be a misunderstanding here. Whatever you've been told, I can't carry you. It's against health and safety codes. I'm happy to go and find the residential manager and ask her for a basin that I can fill with some lukewarm water and then try and wipe you down with a washcloth, but you're going to need more than just this commode for me to properly do my job."

Holy smokes, I thought. Before Two threw the rule book at me, I was about to tell her that the commode chair had reminded me that along with showering I needed to relieve myself as well, as it had been days since I last went. Now asking Two if I could make a number two was out of the question. I was left with no choice but to compress my bowels, an uncomfortable alternative. This was the law of the land, apparently: her back trumped my abdomen. This was thoroughly disappointing. I was accustomed to stifling my needs to get through a flight or a full day of errands, normal, everyday things. I thought that living on my own terms in my own room at Oxford would be my release, an opportunity to let go, to unclench in more ways than one. But now, in this small, dank dorm, caught in a stalemate with my own care aide, I felt like I'd been tapped on the shoulder and awoken from a fantasy of ease and comfort.

Two continued, her unknowingly sadistic adherence to the letter of the law leaving me feeling sick to my bloated stomach. "For starters, you're going to need the university to get you a hoist," she said. I knew precisely what she meant, but the way she phrased it was misleading. The word "hoist," known stateside as a hoyer lift, was a euphemistic disguise, hiding the true nature of the contraption and how it operated. In reality, it was nothing more than a crane—a mechanical beast with an aluminum claw and a sling that the aide would use to transport their clients from wheelchairs onto commode chairs and toilet seats. While some of my disabled siblings might share my visceral contempt for this device, others might view it as a necessary evil—a means to an end. After all, the hoyer lift had been invented by Ted Hoyer, a quadriplegic, who sought to take agency over his own mobility. Though laudable, this 1950s invention was not commensurate with the active life of a disabled student in the year 2016. Regardless of personal opinion, there was no denying how I felt about the raw, physical reality of the hoist: a cold, inanimate tool that reduced my body to a mere object, dangling naked and helpless from a giant crowbar.

From my experience, though, this device makes no one's life easier. The process of strapping someone in and out of the sling can be particularly time-consuming for an aide working on the clock, but most important, for me as the client, being required to swing through the air like that has often felt borderline degrading. I also found that it forced one to have a circumscribed life. I often wondered: What if I wanted to spend the night in a hotel or travel abroad? What would happen then? The answer would be, *Well, you can't because there's no hoist where you want to travel to.*

"A hoist," I repeated, unable to hide my stank face.

Two nodded. "There are other things you'll need too. I'll make a list so you can share it with the care agency and the university first thing in the morning. The day's pretty much over," she said, as she inspected her watch. "Right, I'm going to pop out for a bit and see if I can find a basin for you. Are you going to be okay if I leave you for a while?"

I spaced out for a brief moment, taken aback by the disappointment of my experience so far. Within a span of half a day I'd been shuttled between care aides like a young person who'd fallen through the cracks of the foster care system, and now I was being prevented from using the bathroom. This was so not what I'd expected. My eyes directed me to the bottle of bubbly on the floor next to my luggage. *So much for a celebratory toast,* I thought. "Yeah, I'll be fine, but before you go, could you pour some of that into the flask that's in my bag and place it on the table for me?"

Sipping Dom Pérignon Through a Straw

Two situated me at the desk that overlooked the court-yard and placed my flask, filled with the sparkling wine, on it, close enough for me to drink unaided. All I needed to do was bend down and suck the spout at the lip of the flask. As soon as she left me in peace, I did exactly that. Unbothered by the warm fizz, I swirled the wine around in my mouth, closing my eyes as I swallowed it. My eyes were wet with tears when I opened them. *Why does this all feel like the biggest anticlimax ever?* I thought.

Warmed only by the company of my drink, I gazed out the window at my upright counterparts and lamented over the effortless way they sauntered across the college grounds. They exuded a carefree ease, reveling in the brilliance of their achievements, free from my personal plague of existential concerns.

I was living a life with a degenerative disability, a life that I was determined to live fully. That to me merited a special form of recognition akin to the honors bestowed upon military officers for their sacrifices on the frontline. In my mind, I was a soldier, constantly laying my body on the line in the ongoing battle against ableism.

Every student had their own silent struggles, of course, but despite doing everything my peers had done to get to the same station—and more—our paths felt permanently diverged, and I was bound to be on this ragged, grueling, and considerably isolating course. I knew I deserved better—at the very least, a caregiver who acknowledged and catered to my unique needs.

I knew it was possible. I'd lived with Lucky's affirming care, however messy, and therefore was convinced that the day's divergence was a mere detour on the road to something greater. There was no plan B.

"KNOCK, KNOCK," TWO ANNOUNCED, FROM the doorway. She'd been gone so long that late afternoon had turned into early evening. "So, great news, I found a basin." Two grinned triumphantly as she brandished what very likely was the grubbiest-looking bucket I'd ever seen. It was a salmon-brownish color, no more than twelve inches wide and four or five inches deep. I was less than enthused. I thought of asking her where she'd found it but opted to hold my tongue. For the sake of my blood pressure it was probably best I did not know. "Also, look who I found," Two added. A middle-aged woman wearing a janitor's uniform circled her way around Two and stood beside her. "This is Esther. She's from Uganda. I bumped into her in the hallway mopping the floors. I told her about our situation, and she very kindly offered to help me transfer you onto the bed." Yet another stranger I was expected to open up to and unequivocally embrace within seconds of being introduced. "Thank you for doing this, ma'am," I said, smiling through the sense of resignation and annoyance I felt so I wouldn't be mistaken for being entitled or ungrateful.

"Happy to help, my dear," Esther said. "I don't have much time, though. I need to catch the bus home. I still need to prepare dinner for my husband and the kids." I'd now become desensitized to having my body negotiated over, so without flinching, I let Two and Esther encircle me as if they were inspecting a shipment. Two had forgotten the steps One had shown her. Though slightly tipsy, I proceeded to talk Esther through the technique of lifting me. "On three," Esther said, wiggling herself into position in preparation to cradle me. "One, two...woopah." She scooped me up and nearly swung me across the room toward my bed. "Ah," she exclaimed, "the young man's light as a feather!" I wished she'd been able to transfer me onto a toilet so I'd have been able to relieve myself, but that seemed like a request beyond the scope of what was permissible to ask someone, a stranger for that matter, who was merely extending a favor.

With Esther gone, Two sprung into action and swiftly commenced the bed bath, a procedure that had always been anathema to me. It was a last resort in emergency situations, when a proper bathroom was out of reach, but in the realm of the home-based-care sector, it was a customary procedure. I had always made it crystal clear to every care aide that wiping me down with a face towel could never replace the blissful feeling of running water. The mere thought of having to endure this mode of cleanliness every day for the foreseeable future filled me with an arresting dread.

Two undressed me out of the slim fit Levi's, button-up shirt, argyle sweater vest, and polka-dot tie I'd been wearing. As Two began to wipe me down, I counted the number of times she went over the same spot. The clinical scent of soap and the rough towel against my skin unsettled me. Thank god I was tipsy and desensitized to the absurdity of the situation.

Afterward, I had no choice but to remain there on the bed. It must've been only eight o'clock, but despite my nocturnal nature and because Two couldn't transfer me back into my chair, I was content to call it a day. She changed me into my pajamas. She then proceeded to crouch down beside me as I lay in bed on my side ready to be tucked in. "Just to confirm," Two said, as she drew the sheet and comforter over me. "I turn you every two hours, right?"

"Yep!" I said. If Two didn't turn me every two hours, then pressure buildup around the joints would result in the erosion of the skin and the development of bed sores. "Don't forget me," I appealed to her with enlarged eyes to discourage neglect of this crucial responsibility.

Two smiled reassuringly and said, "Okay, see you in two hours then." A feeling of trust enveloped my body, as if another cozy layer of linen had just been thrown over me. This was the first bit of security I'd felt in the last thirty-six or so hours. Then she heaved herself up from the ground and began swaying her hips toward the door. "Sweet dreams," Two said, flicking the light switch and shutting the door behind her as she exited.

These are just teething problems, I thought, as I lay there in the dark reflecting on the migraine-inducing day I'd had.

Sipping Dom Pérignon Through a Straw

Reminding myself of my own fortitude, it struck me that I'd gritted my teeth through more than a contracted digestive tract in the past. *I've got this*, I convinced myself. But if this was Oxford day one, I'd have to face the rest head-on if I wanted to claim my place here as the powerful, revolutionary force I knew myself to be. *Break the rearview mirror and don't look back, Eddie*, I whispered. *You're here now.* In a span of less than a minute, my mumbled affirmations buckled under the weight of my eyelids, and before I knew it, I had passed out.

A SAVORY METALLIC STALENESS. A SUDDEN throbbing pain on the left side of my body. That's what I tasted and felt as I struggled to orient myself in the dark. Awoken by my hip sizzling and the inner walls of my mouth gnawed to shreds, I put two and two together. I swallowed a ball of phlegm lodged in my throat from the stress of lying on one side all night. Desperate for assistance, I proceeded to call out Two's name. Then I yelled her name. I waited...nothing. *Two forgot me. The bitch forgot me.* This was my red line. I could let everything else slide but not this.

As the son of a registered nurse who'd often lamented the lack of good quality healthcare for communities living on the margins of society, I'd always known that every bedsore's origin story could be traced to an experience of neglect. And I knew that the reason that I'd never had a bedsore after all these years, not even a pimple on my backside, was because for nearly two decades, Mom had slept with one eye open, making sure that I was turned every two hours without fail. I'd never been neglected. So I'd be damned if I let that happen now. I screamed some more. This time with the ferocity of a banshee. Still nothing.

It suddenly clicked, after I'd exhaled sharply, that it was unlikely that Two would be able to hear anything through the prehistoric stone-clad walls that had made this building such a marvel to look at from the outside. Feeling imprisoned and helpless within the confines of the impenetrable concrete, I started hyperventilating from anxiety, but I knew that if I continued to work myself up I'd eventually have a claustrophobia-induced panic attack. *Right, Eddie. Breathe, just breathe. You're alive. You're still alive.* I used what little strength I had to wiggle my body to redistribute some of the pressure that had been nibbling away at my hip. My anguished twitching made things worse as the comforter unexpectedly crept up over my face. "What the fucking fuck!" I cried to the heavens above. Now in tears and feeling defeated, I channeled my breathing through the sliver of an opening in the blankets somewhere near my ear. I just kept breathing. I breathed and breathed and breathed, until the repetitive heaving of my chest eventually anesthetized me. I was jolted awake again by the thud of the door as it swung open and smacked the wall.

"Eddie, oh dear god, I am so sorry," I heard Two say into the dark. I lay there under the heap of polyester bedding, spectacularly exhausted despite hours of so-called sleep, my body zinging with pins and needles. "I don't know what happened. I set my alarm for every two hours, but for some reason it didn't ring," she said. Then Two ripped the covers off of me. "You're drenched," she shrieked.

EIGHT

MAKING OUR WAY ACROSS THE college's courtyard, I was struck by how unforgiving the colder conditions were to the surrounding vegetation. A month had passed since the eventful start to my life as an Oxford master's candidate. It was as if winter had arrived with the sole intention of zapping the vitality and cheer from the charming roses that lined the grounds. If I could, I would have gladly loaned the gardens some of my joy. As far as I was concerned, nothing could have dampened my spirits, not even the treacherous cobblestone walkways, which I'd slowly been adapting to—but which on most days I still found challenging to navigate. I couldn't have been happier, as I was moving out of Margaret Thatcher's grim room—that vortex of melancholy—into a space that was hopefully going to be more soul nourishing. Renovations were only just completed on the dormitory building I'd been waiting to move into all this time, the one with the wheelchair-friendly room I'd initially been assigned. I was now being escorted toward my new living quarters by one of the college representatives.

After some chitchat en route to the refurbished dorms, my escort revealed her curiosity. "She seemed like such a nice girl," she said. *You're not wrong,* I thought, applying more pressure to my joystick as I tried to match her brisk pace. Indeed, Two seemed like a lovely person. Perhaps in another time and place we could have even been friends. But as my care aide? She just didn't cut it. Several days after the incident in which Two had failed to turn me during the course of my sleep, I requested that the care agency swap her out for someone else. Initially, notwithstanding how traumatic that incident had been for me, I was prepared to put the matter behind me and give her another chance. Soon thereafter, however, I began witnessing a pattern of behavior that made me think twice about whether she'd be able to fulfill the role of my right-hand woman. Two much preferred being hands-off. She'd demonstrated an unwillingness to roll up her sleeves and do the actual work of caregiving. Taking advantage of Esther's generosity of spirit, Two had turned what started out as a favor into a permanent arrangement in which Esther was expected to continue doing all my transfers. Lifting me had suddenly become part of her job description, in addition to keeping the dormitory hallways in livable condition. Esther's build wasn't all that different from Two's, stout and soft, so in those first few days I often wondered, *If she can carry me, why can't you?* Worse, Two didn't seem to see anything wrong in outsourcing her duties to a third party. This, coupled with a penchant for gleefully taking inventory of what was or wasn't in compliance with protocol, had me doubting whether she was actually committed to this work.

I had hit my breaking point with Two's reluctance to color outside the lines of compliance and move beyond the bare minimum when one night I caught her rolling her eyes at me. It had been a long day and I was feeling sweaty and sticky, so before going to bed I'd asked her if she wouldn't mind wiping me down. Not in the mood to expend additional energy, Two tried to convince me to go to bed in the grubby state I was in, saying, "You look tired. Don't you just want to go to bed and I'll wipe you down in the morning?" I was having none of it. It was bad enough that I hadn't had a shower in twenty-nine days. The hoist that Two had made the university order was still being shipped. I insisted, pushing back against her pushback. I guess Two didn't take kindly to me asking her to do her job, as she proceeded to make her displeasure known with a spicy eye roll. I didn't say anything. I didn't have to. I'd already made up my mind. Two's days were officially numbered.

"She was," I said to the rep, maintaining Two's dignity more than she had mine. "But unfortunately, it didn't work out."

Trotting alongside me, the college representative folded

her arms, as if her entangled limbs were enough to shield her from the persistent windchill. "I see," she said, pencil-thin brows raised. I could tell by the inflection that she was dying to know more, but I didn't take the bait. Eager to redirect my energies to the positive developments in my life, namely the excitement I was feeling about the new space awaiting me, I kept driving. Still curious, she asked, "What about the other guy I've been seeing helping you around the college? I take it that it didn't work out with him either?"

I shook my head and said, "Nope, unfortunately not."

Two's replacement, Three, was an older man, likely in his mid- to late fifties, who looked a bit like a plump Che Guevara with the beret he wore pretty much around the clock. He, too, didn't make it beyond the two-week mark. Three, though, had left of his own accord. As frustrating as it was to see him go, especially so soon after Two's dismissal, I appreciated him for having the self-awareness to establish right off the bat that he didn't have what it took to do the job. In fact, as he had explained it to me, my case inadvertently redefined the way he began to conceptualize his calling as a care aide.

"We don't work with people like you," Three said to me one morning. He'd found himself physically struggling to move fast enough to get me out the door on time for my first class of the day. As he panted over me and splattered droplets of saliva in my face while trying to feed my arms through my jacket, he said, in a restrained fit of exasperation, "Listen, I never thought I'd see the day when I'd meet a physically challenged individual who does more with his life than me. We work with old white people who lie in bed all day. The highlight of their day is going out for their daily walk around the block. They're trying to slow down while you're trying to ramp up. You're going to school every day, living an active life. And you need us to keep up. I'm not sure I can."

Three helped put the frustration and discontent I'd been bottling up into perspective. I was beginning to think that perhaps I had been the problem. That maybe I'd been asking too much. But in listening to Three vent, it struck me that the problem perhaps lay squarely with an upright system incapable of making room for nonupright success. I was therefore an outlier, forcing my way into recognition with the pioneering nature of my existence. Consequently, the answer wasn't to hold back in terms of voicing my needs but to demand more institutional support. I mean, how else was I going to carry out a full course load and carve out a meaningful and inspiring graduate experience?

When Three subsequently expressed his desire to be redeployed to a more traditional case, I had a deeper conversation with the care agency. They recognized that maybe this was a case too demanding for one person to handle. Together, we reevaluated my care plan, and it was decided that moving forward, instead of one care aide, I'd be assigned two, someone for the daytime and someone for the evenings. I wasn't sure what the financial implications of the new arrangement would be. But given that it didn't come up in my discussions with the agency, I figured that the £10,000 I still had left over from #OxfordEddiecated would be able to see me through for several more months while I continued to work with the agency to firm up my care plan. After all, I was already here. If I was going to need more funding down the line, then surely among the agency, Oxford, and me, we'd be able to figure something out. In the meantime, the most important thing was to put the conditions in place for a successful graduate experience. I didn't travel halfway across the world to spend my time worrying about my day-to-day survival. I came here to live a life of the mind, sharpen my public policy prowess, and dwell in the success of my achievements.

Three was replaced with Four and Five, both of whom were now straggling behind me and the college representative as we approached ROQ West, the most modern-looking building on the Somerville grounds. With its geometric shapes, reminiscent of seventies architecture, the edifice ahead of us looked out of place against the backdrop of the university's medieval aesthetic.

"Sorry to hear that it didn't work out with either of them, but I'm sure you're in good hands with these two," the college representative said, as she ever so slightly tilted her head over her shoulder, acknowledging Four and Five, who were engaged in a conversation of their own as we entered ROQ West.

"I hope so," I responded. The last month had illuminated in real time just how complicated an endeavor it was going to be to juggle student life with the logistics of my day-to-day care and overall reasonable accommodation requirements.

The college rep gripped a doorknob after leading us down a long, echoing hallway. And as she began to turn it, I held my breath in anticipation.

"All right, Eddie, welcome to your new room," she said, opening the door.

The airiness of this new space was such a welcome relief from the gloominess I'd grown accustomed to. I wheeled myself through the door. Unable to help myself, I immediately cracked a smile. "Sorry it's taken us a few weeks to get your new room ready for you. Hopefully you'll find it more suitable for your needs," the college rep said from behind me in the entryway.

Somewhat awestruck, I propelled myself a little further into the room. Then, in appreciation for the spaciousness that greeted me, I spun myself around in doughnut formations across the middle of the room. The skid marks I was imprinting into the carpet functioned in a way to circumscribe this space as my own. Indeed, it was my ability to navigate my wheelchair freely throughout the room that had immediately sealed it for me. "This is more like it," I exclaimed. Giddy, the appreciation I felt could entirely be attributed to the dimensions rather than the aesthetics of the space. Because, to be perfectly honest, with the adjustable hospital bed on the left wall as the room's decorative centerpiece, my surroundings looked more like a private ICU room than the dorm room of a graduate student. There was nothing visually appealing about my new space. But in exchange for greater freedom of movement I figured the anemic interior would be a tolerable compromise. Facing Four and Five as they lurked in the doorway with blank faces, I flashed a broad grin, corralling them into the room with an encouraging nod.

As I continued to survey my new abode, the college rep slunk her way from the edge of the room toward the door across from the hospital bed. "And here we have your bathroom," she said as she pushed it open. We congregated near the entrance, huddling together to take a peek inside. There, the crane I'd been waiting for with bated breath stood resolutely. It took up virtually the entire surface area of the floor, its imposing bulk blocking the streaks of light that poured into the bathroom from the main room.

Inspecting the hoist from top to bottom I surveyed its features, squinting at it with a tinge of disgust. I sat there, my stomach twisting in shame as I realized it had been several weeks since my last bowel movement. The ban on aides transferring me had made it next to impossible to relieve myself, and of course the delay in the hoist's delivery had only made matters worse.

Despite my reservations, it seemed Four and Five were pleased that the hoist was now available. While reviewing my care plan with the agency, I discovered that according to the UK's Health and Safety guidelines, a single care aide was not permitted to operate a hoist alone—yet another reason why it had become imperative that two care aides be assigned to my care plan. *I hope this entire degree is worth my indignity,* I thought. Either way, I had to suck it up then and there and make peace with the fact that for the next year this device was going to be a key component in the operationalization of my life. Otherwise, I'd spend the whole time being victimized by an inanimate object. *It is what it is,* I thought, shrugging my shoulders in resignation.

As the college rep was in the process of wrapping up her tour of my new bathroom, I heard a thud on the window from behind me in the bedroom. Then I heard the sound of muffled voices, which was quickly followed by more knocking. Curious, I backed out of the doorway of the bathroom and maneuvered myself closer to the window. Through the blinds, I saw the silhouettes of the noisemakers. "Eddie, it's us." The squad was here.

My friendship with the squad was the one thing about my new life as an Oxford grad student that hadn't gone pear shaped in the last month. Formed in the first few days of orientation, our friendship group comprised five of us who'd graduated from the African Leadership Academy and had been admitted into Oxford. That we all ended up here—and in the same program no less—wasn't entirely surprising. In the six years since I'd graduated from the inaugural class, the Academy had quickly gained a worldwide reputation for being a hotbed of talent, churning out the continent's brightest and most accomplished young people. With an embarrassment of riches, the boarding school quickly became a feeder of applicants for spots in the world's top universities in search of African candidates to diversify their student body. In the months leading up to my admission to Oxford, I'd heard through the grapevine that a bunch of us had applied to the master's program in public policy. I had no clue who the other alums were who'd also been admitted until we bumped into each other on the first day of orientation several weeks ago.

I'd been feeling so unmoored—so profoundly lonely—that when I saw my friends on the first day of the official welcome to the program, I found myself clinging to them almost instantly. Though we weren't particularly close in boarding school, it was as if I'd been reunited with long-lost relatives. There was Tebello, affectionately called Tebs. Hailing from the Kingdom of Lesotho, which he constantly felt compelled to remind people was a country landlocked within South Africa, Tebs was one year below me at the Academy and eventually went on to graduate from Stanford. Tebs was someone who oozed *je ne sais quoi*. A foodie, a fashionista, a connoisseur of literary fiction, he was so refined that he might as well have been a cultural critic for a major lifestyle magazine. I related the most to Tebs, as he too was a queer Black man trying to carve out a space of love and beauty for himself in the world.

Then there was Jessica, or Jess. With a megawatt smile that illuminated every space she occupied and a razor-sharp mind that could slice through the most complex of discourses, she was quite possibly the only person I'd ever met who truly was equal parts beauty and brains. A proud export of the land of a thousand hills, Rwanda, Jess was in Tebs's year when we were together in boarding school and has always had an abiding passion for health sciences. She seemed to be someone who was fiercely loyal—the kind of friend who'd place herself on the battlefield in a fight against one's haters.

There was Aïda, our towering Black feminist intellectual from Senegal. We both graduated from the inaugural class of ALA and later found ourselves both attending undergrad in Canada—she at Quest and I at Carleton. I deeply admired her for her ability to honor the multiplicity of identities and experiences she embodied. Refusing to be pigeonholed, she was simultaneously Muslim, a global citizen, a pan-Africanist, and an unrepentant champion of social justice, as well as someone perfectly at home navigating institutional life. She'd joke that she, like me, was a corporate girl by day and a critic of the neoliberal establishment by night.

Finally, Vivian, our God-fearing soul sistah we affectionately referred to as Auntie Viv. Technically, she didn't attend ALA as a student. She came to the Academy after graduating from Georgetown in Washington, DC, to work in the student relations department. We considered her an honorary ALA alum. Viv was a deep thinker and an inspiring poet. Like me, she was also Namibian by birth and African by destiny. Unbeknownst to all of them, they'd suddenly become my anchor of safety in an environment that had started to fall short of my expectations. They were my portal to joy, an escape from that sinking feeling I was experiencing in my private life in the dorms. In those first few days familiarizing ourselves with life in the small city as newly minted Oxford grad students, we'd found home in one another, calling ourselves "the squad" and vowing to stick together for the entirety of our time there.

"I'm coming!" I shouted back, bursting at the seams from excitement. We'd planned to spend the day together, catching a movie and then going out for dinner.

"I take it you need to head out?" the college rep said.

I nodded enthusiastically. "Yeah, I have plans with my friends," I replied.

"Great, well, I won't keep you much longer then. But just to confirm before you head out, we've assigned you two additional rooms—for each of your care aides." Then, turning to face Four and Five, she said, "I don't know which of you is doing days and which of you nights. But for the one doing the night shift, you'll get the room right next door. The person working the day shift will get a room in the dormitory building across from this one." Four, a petite woman from Senegal who spoke with a heavy French accent, had been assigned nights. Because she needed to be close by to move back and forth for my turns, she was going to be the one to snatch up the room next door. I didn't really need Five all that much once I had been bathed and dressed for the day. I attended lectures during the day and could therefore rely on my classmates and notetaker for assistance in sipping a coffee or with retrieving books from the backpack strapped behind my chair.

Except, of course, if I needed to pee, in which case, I'd just call him to meet me back at the dorms between breaks. So it made sense that he would take the room farther away. Five, a burly man from Tanzania had an antisocial streak about him. And with his inability to give more than one-word answers when engaging in conversation, he seemed like the kind of guy who actually preferred having as limited contact with his clients as possible anyway.

The college rep handed them each a set of keys. "Other than that, you're all set to go, Eddie," the college rep said. She leaned down and gave me an awkward hug, and then we all made our way out through the main door.

I took inventory of my new space, mentally checking off each item to ensure nothing was out of place. Satisfied with my assessment, I made my way toward the door, eager to join my friends.

As I propelled myself forward, I heard a loud chime coming from my backpack, which was securely fastened on the back of my chair. My phone was notifying me of a new message. "Just a moment," I murmured to myself, stopping in my tracks.

I enlisted Four, who was closest, to retrieve my phone. With nimble fingers, she whipped the device out of my backpack and held it up to me. Using facial recognition, the screen unlocked, and an email from the care agency appeared, arousing my curiosity.

"Dear Mr. Ndopu, based on our revised calculations, below

is a breakdown of the total cost for your care over the next year..."

With each passing line, my eyes widened, barely able to believe what I was reading. "Oh my God, oh my God, oh my God," I murmured to myself, overwhelmed by the news. The itemized bill now reflected One's "On the Ground" services, Two and Three's overtime pay, and the cost of an additional care aide as per my amended care plan. The total balance was now a jaw-dropping £66,000, due in twelve weeks' time.

"Is everything okay?" Four asked, looking at me with concern. Despite having scraped together enough money to make it to Oxford, I had never imagined that the #OxfordEddiecated funds I had worked so tirelessly to raise would be eaten up so quickly. Suddenly my friends' eager knocking at the window sounded more like the care agency knocking at the door, its hand outstretched, saying "pay up." I must have looked horrified. Primed to conceal my true feelings, I resigned to press on. "Um...yeah, I'm fine," I stammered.

Four nodded and returned my phone to my backpack. We exited the room, each heading in separate directions. She and Five turned right, heading toward their respective quarters, and I veered left toward the main entrance and the comforting embrace of my new friends. Inhaling deeply, I reminded myself to put any anxieties about the future aside and focus on discovering Oxford and making unforgettable memories with my squad. I could deal with the money later.

The late afternoon sun hung low, casting a golden glow

across the college grounds as I emerged outside. The squad cackled, playfully pushing each other, their laughter carrying through the air. They cheered as soon as they caught sight of me, as if they'd seen Britney herself. "Eddie! Ready to have a good time?" Viv asked with great jubilation and contagious excitement.

We began our stroll into town, the bustling streets alive with activity. As we walked, we chatted and laughed, taking in the sights and sounds around us. Eventually, we decided to go see *La La Land* to determine for ourselves whether the film, starring Ryan Gosling and Emma Stone, was worth the hype. When we arrived at the movie theater, we weaved through the lines and made our way to the front of the ticket station, where we requested a wheelchair-accessible seat. The man behind the high counter peered over and squinted at us, his expression showing a hint of annoyance at the interruption to his phone game. He took inventory of my presence, his gaze lingering on my wheelchair before he heaved a deep sigh. Without even pausing to greet us, he informed us that the main auditorium where the film was being screened was unfortunately not wheelchair accessible.

I furrowed my brow in confusion. How was it possible for a modern cinema to be inaccessible? "This is unacceptable," I said firmly.

The man responded by nearly ejecting the neon green gum that swirled around in his mouth.

"I can offer you Moana," he said, his voice fried by the

speaker he spoke through, nodding at the movie poster behind him.

I was stunned and couldn't help but wonder if he was serious. "*Moana*? The animated film?" He nodded. I could tell by his intransigence that he thought my incredulity was me somehow going overboard. Little did he realize that his "chill, bro, it's not that deep" attitude was exactly why inaccessibility is so often viewed as something unfortunate rather than as a manifestation of injustice and exclusion of nonuprights. It absolutely was that deep.

"But we came to see *La La Land*," Jess said with simmering frustration. The employee shrugged.

"Forget it. Let's go to Turtle Bay instead," I said to the squad, wheeling myself away from further rejection.

As we began walking out in protest, Viv wagged her finger in the guy's face and said, "When you lose a disabled customer, you lose their friends and loved ones too. I'm not coming back here again. And I'll make sure everyone I know doesn't come either."

We left the movie theater, and though we held our heads high, I was still outraged. I deeply wished I could have been able to move through the world without feeling as though I were constantly fighting ableism at every turn. As if structural barriers were not a hundred feet high, something as simple as enjoying a movie seemed impossible. I was fed up that even on my day off I still had to be switched on. I still needed to advocate for my right to occupy space. "Sorry for zipping away like that, guys," I said, worried that perhaps I'd misdirected the multilayered outrage I was feeling at my friends by speeding off.

"What? Don't be silly, babe, you have nothing to be sorry about," Jess reassured me. "It's ridiculous that in the year 2016 a movie theater in a vibrant university town like this can't accommodate someone in a wheelchair. You have every right to feel angry."

Then Aïda chimed in, "Seriously, what is the message they're sending? People with disabilities don't have the right to go out and have fun?"

Feeling validated, I smiled. "Well, we're not gonna let that ruin our day. We're still young, gifted, and Black," I said.

Tebs, theatrical as ever, started belting out the rest of the lyrics: "Oh what a lovely precious dream."

"Um, stick to your day job, boo," Jess chirped, sending us all into raucous laughter.

We soon found ourselves walking down an alleyway toward our final stop. Tucked in the corner at the end of the narrow street, next to a wall covered in graffiti, was Turtle Bay, a Jamaican restaurant we'd recently discovered. We walked inside the hidden gem and planted ourselves at a table farthest from the traffic.

"Thanks, guys, for having my back earlier," I said, as soon as we got comfortable. "So grateful to have you guys in my life. Isn't it amazing that we all ended up here together?"

Indeed, it truly was. And to think that had I not forced

my way into ALA several years earlier I would not be here now, benefiting from this friendship I so desperately needed. Though Chris, one of the school's founders, had said to me that I was "one of a kind" at the end of the finalist weekend I thought I'd aced, I returned home only to receive a call several weeks later informing me that my admission had been unsuccessful. When I pressed the admissions officer charged with conveying the news to me for an answer as to why, she'd taken a pregnant pause and said, "We think you are exceptional. It's just that, at this juncture, we don't feel completely confident in our ability to effectively meet your needs."

I was shattered. Then, days after, Mom wrote an email on my behalf to the founders congratulating them on bringing the vision of this preparatory school for Africa's future world leaders to life, thinking that she was somehow helping me to move on. She had apparently even concluded her correspondence by wishing the incoming class well. "I wanted them to know that there are no hard feelings," Mom told me.

I was livid. No hard feelings? *Are you kidding me! Of course there are hard feelings,* I thought in response. This was not the time to be gracious. This was the time to push back against the idea that my disability had made me ineligible for admission. Refusing to accept the outcome, I went behind Mom's back and wrote a letter of my own. Back then I still had enough strength and dexterity in my hands to physically type on a keyboard, feed myself, and hold a phone, though these kinds of activities had begun to feel increasingly tiring.

Nevertheless, using three or four of my best fingers, I hijacked a desktop computer in the library of the high school I was attending at the time and began pouring my soul onto the page. Defiant, I informed the founders, as diplomatically as I knew how at age sixteen, that they had made a big mistake. I invited them to reconsider their decision and understand that it was in their own interest to do so. Should I one day go on to change the world, they would get the credit for having taken a chance on the disabled kid with big dreams. I knew it was a long shot. But I hit send anyway, if for nothing else than to remind myself of the tenacity that had gotten me there in the first place.

A month later, on a lazy Sunday afternoon, as I was lounging and mindlessly watching MTV, Mom waltzed into the living room and said, "There's a call for you."

It was Fred, ALA's other cofounder. "Thank you for your letter, Edward," he said matter-of-factly. "We'd like to offer you a place in the inaugural class of the African Leadership Academy."

"You know, when I first heard I'd be in the same program as you," Jess said, also in a reflective mood apparently, "I didn't know what you'd be like. You have this celebrity status. Every time I go on Facebook I see pictures of you speaking at fancy conferences and posing with world leaders. I thought I was going to meet a diva, but you're actually incredibly sweet."

I was simultaneously flattered and embarrassed. It was then that the server arrived, saving me from having to respond.

"What can I get you guys?" she asked, her ballpoint pen in one hand, poised against a notepad clasped in the other.

"We're all doing the jerk chicken with rice and peas," Viv said as she stacked the menus up on top of each other, handing them over to the server.

"Our signature dish. Can't go wrong with that...I'll be back in a jiffy with your orders," the server said.

"If I was a celebrity I'd have had better lighting when this headshot was taken," Tebs said, fiddling with his lanyard and inspecting his student card. "This is such an unflattering picture."

"Bruh, it can't be as bad as mine," Viv chimed in, reaching for hers in her wallet.

"Let's compare," Aïda said, retrieving hers as well while laughing hysterically.

Gently, Tebs removed the lanyard from around my neck. Then he placed my student card down on the table next to everyone else's.

"Mine looks like a mug shot," Aïda joked. I let out a hearty laugh. Then, gazing down at my student card on the table, my jovial grin collapsed into a pensive sliver of a smile. The black, bold letters jumped out at me like a revelation in scripture: EDWARD NDOPU.

Strange. I hadn't thought about my father, my namesake, in years. Wonga and I had been estranged from Dad since we were five and six, respectively.

Dad was among a handful of journalists calling for racial

justice in present-day Namibia, the country of my birth, who tragically found themselves as collateral damage in a vicious political climate. To this day, few historians speak about the harrowing dark pits in neighboring Angola, which sought to vanquish the comrades who had been accused of spying on behalf of the Apartheid regime. Brothers-in-arms were turned against each other at the peak of the fight for independence and the struggle for freedom. Suspected of being a counter-revolutionary agent, he was subsequently thrown into the dungeons of Lubango.

Dad had been among those who'd languished in captivity in the period before Namibian independence, which was eventually attained in 1990, the year I was born. My heart bled for what he must have gone through. I never held him responsible for the pain that had been inflicted on him, but I've always held him responsible for the pain he inflicted on us as a family. He was a victim of injustice; this I could not deny. But his refusal to work through his inner demons and previous traumas from his imprisonment and probably even before then made him a shitty father to Wonga and me and an even shittier husband to Mom. He was an absent father from the outset, devoting his attention and affection to booze instead of his family. In the years leading up to Mom's divorce from Dad, he had been neglectful and physically and psychologically abusive—beating Mom to a pulp before she eventually found the strength to leave him, not taking us to school even once during the few times Wonga and I found ourselves in his care, and, in later years, failing to pay even a cent toward our upkeep as his children. For reasons only he knows, he chose to transfer the violence he'd suffered rather than transform it. That's on him.

By this point, Dad's contribution to my life had barely amounted to a footnote, if that. But as I glanced down, my memories tracing the shape of my name on the lanyard, I couldn't help but think of him, the original Edward Ndopu. And even though he was a father in name only, I still chose to name myself after him, a decision I'd taken when I was nine going on ten.

Mom had just relocated us from Namibia to South Africa. Her decision to return to her birth country was partly because Namibia, the country she had been in solidarity with since she was a young nurse in her twenties, had begun to see her as a foreign national in the postindependence scramble for the best jobs. With narrowing career prospects for our upward financial mobility, now as a family of three in Windhoek, Mom was left with no choice but to take up work in Cape Town. But I'd always had a hunch that her decision to move Wonga and me was also fueled by a desire to put distance between us and our so-called father.

It was the day before I started third grade. By this point I had been enrolled in mainstream education for well over two years. Wonga and I took a tour of our new school, nestled in Cape Town's sprawling, leafy northern suburbs. Mr. Elbregcht, the principal of the school, graciously played tour guide and led us across the campus, past and up to the building in which

Sipping Dom Pérignon Through a Straw

I would spend the academic year. The red brick structure, with its large, gridded windows, overlooked a manicured courtyard with a sherbet-orange bench sitting along the edge. The bench, with its paint peeling from the dark, archaic wood, must have been as old as the school itself. Mom wheeled me toward the chewed-up bench, leaving Wonga to make small talk with Mr. Elbregcht. She plopped herself down, then wheeled me between her legs so that I wouldn't roll away. "You're a big boy now," she said, ever serious. "Junior is not a name for a big boy. What do you want your new friends and teachers to call you?" she asked. I'd always been Junior, a name that had been given to me as a result of a compromise reached between Mom and Dad rather than as a customary sign of respect for my father. A new name? I'd never considered it.

"What about Khanya?" Mom prodded. Khanya, which means "to shine" or "to be the light" in isiXhosa, our family's ancestral language on Mom's side, was the name she wanted for me at birth. I looked at her and shrugged. The sun radiated that day, and the rays seemed to be nudging me to go along with Khanya. In all honesty, I had begun to see myself more as my mother's son than as my father's, but something about naming myself Khanya didn't feel quite right in my tiny body. I sat for a bit and thought about it, Wonga and Mr. Elbregcht chatting away in the distance. Before I knew it, the answer came surging up to the surface. Feeling serene and certain, I shook my head. "Um, no, Mommy," I said. "I think I'll go with Edward. I want everyone at my new school to call me Edward."

I'd been given a golden opportunity to untether myself from my father entirely, to cement the geographical distance that Mom had created between us and kick-start my journey toward healing from the pain he had inflicted on me. So why, on the cusp of a new grade at a new school—a blank canvas on which to recreate myself—did I choose to keep the name of a man who'd caused so much heartache and misery? That morning, blinking my Bambi eyes into Mom's face, I didn't have the language to articulate my thought process, but the logic has since become clear. My little self had discovered the power of transmutation. If I could evacuate Dad from his own name, then perhaps I would be able to evacuate him from the narrative about the rest of my life. I was succeeding at the thing he had failed to do: transform pain rather than transfer it.

Edward Ndopu was now emblazoned on my Oxford University student card. It was a form of alchemy to hold this problematic name on my tongue and imbue it with new meaning. Although he was the original owner of this name, he had lost his right to own it. The firstborn son, whom he'd abandoned and hurt so systematically, had reclaimed it. When the world heard this name it would now be associated with all that I had accomplished, all that I would become, as if only one Edward Ndopu ever existed.

A hand carrying a plate of food suddenly swooped into focus from my peripheral vision. Tebs yanked the lanyards out of the way, making room on the table for the feast that was about to unfold. "Jerk chicken with rice and peas for you, my dear," the server said as she laid the dish down in front of me. It looked divine, with the golden brown chicken resting on top of fluffy, fragrant rice. Salivating from anticipation, I bent down to inhale the tantalizing aroma of island spices wafting up toward my face while the server went around the table and placed everyone else's orders down in front of them as well.

"I've never been so excited to dig in," Jess said, pulling her plate closer. "It looks so good," Aïda said, equally as ravenous and jubilant.

Viv, seated to my left, looked up at Tebs sitting to my right and said, "Let me feed Eddie."

"Don't worry, Auntie Viv, I got it," Tebs replied.

Not wasting any time, Tebs reached for the cutlery and proceeded to cut my food into manageable pieces. Then he scooped some up onto the fork and fed me my first bite. The chicken was so succulent and soft that it dissolved in my mouth. As I chewed, I watched Tebs stabbing another piece of food onto the fork. He was so engrossed in what he was doing that he completely forgot about himself. Watching him take joy in helping me moved me so deeply.

"This chicken is amazing, man," I said between bites, and everyone nodded in agreement. Jess and Aïda swapped stories about their latest travel adventures, while Viv and Tebs reminisced about old times. The atmosphere was so warm and welcoming that I couldn't help but feel content, both with the food and with the company. These were the moments that made life worth living—the simple pleasures of good food and good company that created lasting memories. It felt so good to be with people who genuinely wanted to assist me, who cared for me wholeheartedly and not begrudgingly.

I can almost hear my charismatic two-year-old self now, passionately making an argument for my undeniable right to more luscious banana puree. Undoubtedly a defining moment for me as I learned the sheer power of my words. Oh, how this photo captures my very essence! I'm sure this was the very first spark of my lifelong journey of speaking up and speaking out.

My mom, an absolute vision of eighties glam, radiating confidence and elegance as she strikes a pose for a beauty pageant sponsored by a local newspaper. Despite living at a time when Black lives were constantly threatened by a harsh and oppressive regime, Mom and her generation refused to let their spirits be broken. Instead, they found ways to carve out space for joy, beauty, and levity, creating a sense of hope and inspiration that continues to shine. This photo is a testament to the indomitable human spirit and a reminder that even in the darkest of times, light and love can always find a way to prevail.

At the ripe old age of twenty, I had already gained some traction in my work advocating for the educational rights of children with disabilities. This photo showcases the flyer for the "Master's Tea" talk I delivered at Yale University. Master's Teas are talks given by renowned experts in their fields to Yale University students. I was honored to be one of the youngest speakers that the Yale student chapter of UNICEF has invited to keynote this event.

There's nothing quite as electrifying as hitting the pavement with like-minded activists, united in a shared passion for human rights. Here I am as a campaigner for Amnesty International, marching alongside fearless defenders on the front lines just months before I embarked on my graduate studies. Little did I know that my next destination, Oxford, would soon become the epicenter of my own personal struggle for freedom and justice.

As a teen, I received a transformative education at the African Leadership Academy in Johannesburg, South Africa. This esteemed boarding school instilled in me not only academic excellence but also a robust sense of confidence in my abilities as a leader. As I look at this lovely photo and reminisce about my graduation day, I'm certain that this experience set me on the path to a life of advocacy.

Love this avant-garde portrait in which I am elegantly draped in a magnificent purple tutu. The photograph is part of a photo exhibition I personally organized to support my own cause, #OxfordEddiecated. With this exhibition, I sought to showcase the beauty and range of disability, celebrate myself in all my technicolor radiance, and use the power of art to inspire change.

Check out this epic snapshot of me and my close-knit crew of friends, drumming up some serious hype for #OxfordEddiecated! We hit up the streets outside a trendy restaurant in downtown Johannesburg and turned heads left and right with our custom-made tees. Shout-out to my boy Adrian for this genius idea—we had supporters flocking to us in no time!

Before I embarked on my journey at Oxford, I attended Carleton University, nestled in the vibrant city of Ottawa, Canada. It was here that I honed my skills, challenged my intellect, and laid the foundation for my future successes. I remember the exhilarating feeling of donning my academic regalia on graduation day, the buzz of excitement in the air, and the sheer joy of being surrounded by my peers, who had become lifelong friends. This photo remains a cherished memento, a testament to the countless hours of hard work and dedication that culminated in one of the proudest moments of my life.

Behold me at my very first drag show in Canada, during my undergrad years! With a hot pink boa draped around my neck, my unbridled joy is palpable in this picture. I felt completely alive and in my element as I soaked up the glittering energy of the performers on stage.

This picture was taken during my very first week as a graduate student at Oxford University. The stunning dome-shaped architecture of the Radcliffe Camera looms impressively behind me, serving as a visual embodiment of the university's scholarly excellence. With a wide smile on my face, I proudly posed for this photo, announcing to the world (and my Facebook friends) that I had officially arrived.

This is one moment at Oxford that was simply euphoric. My heart was bursting with joy as I lay in the soft grass, surrounded by my beloved squad, gazing up at the vast expanse of the sky. Tebs, our trusty photographer, was busy capturing the memory of our laughter, the warmth of the sun on our skin, and the beauty of the world around us.

Tebs, Aïda, our friend Rob, and I are captured bursting in laughter in this shot on the lush grounds of Somerville College. It was a moment of unbridled joy and relief, as we had just wrapped up our grueling Economics exam. With a glint in my eye, I triumphantly declared, "The universe holds the key to the rest."

My dearest friends, Jess and Tebs, and I radiating with joy and excitement mere moments after I had been conferred with my Master of Public Policy degree at Oxford University. My incredible squad, the people who had saved me from the jaws of uncertainty, shared this monumental achievement with me. I attended the graduation ceremony just for them. My degree represents so much more than just an academic accomplishment; it is a testament to the strength of our enduring friendship and the deep affection we hold for one another.

A momentous occasion outside the iconic Sheldonian Theatre in Oxford, where I was enveloped in a warm, affectionate hug from Tebs. In the background, the lovely duo of Jess and Aïda are seen huddling together, their faces exuding pure joy and love. And who could forget the fantastic friend on my right, a mutual pal who came to join in the celebrations and share in the revelry? Of course, it was my dear Auntie Viv, who had the foresight to capture this unforgettable moment on camera.

To commemorate the culmination of my graduate studies at Oxford and the commencement of my personal healing journey, I teamed up with a cohort of brilliant artists and intellectuals of my generation for an awe-inspiring photoshoot. From left to right: Travis Alabanza, Alok Vaid-Menon, me, and Kat Kai Kol-Kes. To me, this was the ultimate graduation and a testament to my perseverance and resilience, a moment when I embodied my most rebellious and radiant self, projecting an aura of defiance and triumph.

Here I am, basking in the warm embrace of the African sun on a picturesque beach in the breathtaking paradise of Mauritius. This moment was truly a gift, a much-needed respite from the demands of everyday life and an opportunity to reflect and heal after graduating from Oxford. This serene environment provided the perfect backdrop for me to rediscover my inner peace with profound gratitude. This was a truly transformative experience that will stay with me for a lifetime.

What a memorable night! I was attending a star-studded fundraiser during New York Fashion Week, reveling in the glamour and glitz of the event. However, the real magic was in the shared purpose held by everyone in the room: to support survivors of sexual assault. It was an honor to be a part of such a meaningful event.

I had the privilege of spending time with a group of wonderful children with disabilities in an inclusive education classroom in a village outside of Kigali. As part of my humanitarian mission, I wanted to highlight the importance of providing equal educational opportunities for children with disabilities. The experience was humbling and inspiring, and it was heartwarming to see the children's eagerness to learn and to grow into their immense potential.

Here I am surrounded by bright young minds from Pioneer Academy in Johannesburg. It was a profound privilege to take part in an event that demystified disability for these curious and open-hearted students. I'm a firm believer that by exposing young people to the rich tapestry of diverse experiences, we can help them develop the formidable empathy muscle that will serve them well as they grow into compassionate and rights-respecting adults.

With the world as my stage, this snapshot captures me during a dress rehearsal for the world-renowned Global Citizen Festival at the iconic FNB Stadium in Johannesburg. Amid the thrilling anticipation of speaking before a crowd of eighty thousand, in an unexpected turn of events, I found myself rubbing shoulders with two comedic legends, Trevor Noah and Dave Chappelle, exchanging laughs and words of encouragement. This photo perfectly encapsulates the electric atmosphere of the festival, where individuals from all walks of life come together to support a common cause and make a positive impact on the world.

I am sitting before a crowd of passionate young activists at the Festival of Action for the Sustainable Development Goals in Bonn, Germany. One of the most rewarding aspects of championing human rights is the true honor that comes with utilizing my voice to magnify the voices of those who face inequality and injustice. These young people are already carving paths towards a brighter future.

Check out this picture of me all dressed up and hitting the red carpet! I was fortunate enough to come across the amazing Kim Jayde, MTV Base's red carpet correspondent, at the world premiere of *MTV Shuga: Down South*. In contrast to the norm, Kim knelt down beside me in her heels (can you believe it?) so that we could have a meaningful and authentic conversation with proper eye contact. Her rare kindness and care truly touched me, and I can confidently say to all members of the press, "Take note: this is how it's done!"

Who would have thought that I'd one day find myself standing shoulder to shoulder with the deputy secretary-general of the United Nations, posing for a photo at the iconic UN headquarters in New York? It's almost too incredible to believe! But there I was, in my role as an advocate for the UN's Sustainable Development Goals, grinning from ear to ear as I appeared alongside this formidable figure, Her Excellency Amina Mohammed. I was beyond grateful for this once-in-a-lifetime opportunity.

Incredible fate smiled upon me just months after I graduated from Oxford. I was attending a grand centenary celebration, held at the Soweto campus of the University of Johannesburg, in honor of the great Nelson Mandela's birth. The pièce de résistance of the event? I was lucky enough to meet the keynote speaker, the one and only Oprah Winfrey. And as if that wasn't enough, the event fell right on my birthday, November 29! Of course, no such encounter would be complete without a stunning snapshot to commemorate the moment!

I was absolutely beside myself sitting next to my beaming mother, posing for what would become an unforgettable picture with none other than the forty-fourth president of the United States, Barack Obama. The adrenaline pumped through my veins so intensely that I felt like I could levitate out of my wheelchair. It was one of those pinch-me moments, yet there I was, the only nonupright in a sea of A-listers. It was a eureka moment, the sudden realization that I had to do something great with this unique and powerful platform that had been given to me.

Rolling in style! This photo captures the moment when I was wheeling myself out of the elevator on my way to New York's Central Park, where I spoke to a crowd of eighty thousand people at that year's Global Citizen Festival. The festival brings together artists, world leaders, and humanitarians from around the world to demand an end to extreme poverty.

Here I am speaking on a panel at the World Economic Forum in Davos. Mere moments prior, I faced a perilous brush with death while navigating the treacherous terrain of the Swiss Alps. Despite the harrowing experience, I was able to compose myself for my talk on accelerating concerted action on the UN's Sustainable Development Goals.

Captured in this photo is the moment just before I wheeled out into the dazzling lights of Manhattan's nightlife. As a proud resident of this iconic city, I can tell you that there's nothing quite like feeling the energy of the Big Apple pulsing through my veins! And of course, to fully embody a night out on the town, one must look their absolute best. So I took great care in choosing my outfit and accessories, making sure to add just the right amount of flair to stand out in the city that never sleeps!

NINE

Near the conclusion of our meal, I noticed a peculiar sensation in my stomach. Initially, I dismissed it, assuming it was the result of overindulging. I had eaten so hurriedly that it felt like I had swallowed my food whole. But as the cramps worsened, I became anxious. *What the hell is happening to me?* I wondered. This wasn't the typical feeling of fullness. My body was starting to revolt against the fact that I hadn't had a bowel movement in several weeks.

"Are you okay, Eddie?" Tebs asked, laying the fork down on the table. I closed my eyes, trying to withstand the pain that was welling up inside me. Auntie Viv chimed in, "Do you need some water?" I shook my head, and the table fell silent, the murmurs of concern weighing heavily in the air.

I knew how to put on a brave face, but embodying true courage eluded me. The public image I had cultivated navigating elite spaces as a humanitarian speaker while putting every school's grading curve to shame contrasted sharply with the private battles I was now fighting. Admitting the truth of my circumstances meant coming face-to-face with the fact that the stability I was projecting wasn't real. This wasn't like not being able to access the movie theater. This was institutional ableism. This was about the mental and physiological trade-offs I had to make to survive in my own body. In this case, how I had to deny myself relief, cruel and unusual punishment in the name of being easy to work with. I was losing control of my life, and I couldn't fathom why I found myself in this situation—let alone expect others to grasp it—and the resulting shame held me back from the bravery I needed to confide in my squad. So I forced a smile and lied through gritted teeth.

Suddenly, a sharp pain shot through me and I winced. "Eddie, we have to get you to the hospital right now," Tebs explained, his face etched in concern. I knew I needed medical attention right away, but I shook my head, still attempting to feign normalcy.

"It's just indigestion," I said. My friends eyed me suspiciously, but they didn't press the matter further. The rest of the meal was strained with awkward silences, and worried glances passed between us.

Sipping Dom Pérignon Through a Straw

As soon as we finished eating, I excused myself. "We'll walk you back," Jess said, already waiving for the check.

"No, I'm good," I responded, determined to leave alone. "I'll catch up with you later." I had Tebs turn my wheelchair on for me, then I backed up, swiveled out sideways, and charged for the door.

The cool air provided some solace as I sped down the road, but every bump amplified the cramps. I applied maximum pressure to my joystick and sped toward Somerville. En route, I instructed Siri to call Five, and I told him to prepare to meet me at the back entrance of the college right away. The cobblestone streets were no match for my wheelchair as I deftly zipped through town, trying to get back as soon as possible.

As I approached the back of the residence hall, my eyes fell upon Five standing impassively by the entrance. My words came tumbling out, "I'm suffering from constipation and need a doctor right away!" But Five's response was tepid and unemotional. Five made no effort to feign empathy. I couldn't afford to waste any more time on his indifference, so I propelled myself forward, wheeling my chair through the entrance with Five trailing behind me.

As we reached my dorm room, I directed Five to call the National Health Services hotline on speakerphone, my mind a maelstrom of anticipation and dread. *What if Tebs is right and I need to go to the hospital?* I was already in serious debt, and even the UK's universal health coverage wouldn't provide a soft landing for my financial free fall.

Five positioned the phone close to my mouth. "Hello, I need a physician for an emergency house call. It's urgent."

FOUR SAT DIAGONALLY ACROSS FROM me, perched at the edge of my bed. I watched her resist the urge to yawn, feeling guilty that I'd had her awakened from her preshift slumber. But duty called. I needed her to be on hand to assist Five in case the doctor wanted me transferred out of my wheelchair to properly examine me. The front door of my room stood partially open for the doctor.

After what felt like hours of stomach churning, a figure finally poked their head around the door and shouted, "House call?" The person spilled into the doorway from the corridor and had scraggly black hair with streaks of grey.

"Yes," I replied, relieved that a physician had finally been dispatched to my aid. The only thing that gave him away as a clinician was the stethoscope dangling from his neck. He could otherwise have passed for a handyman with the way he carried a canvas duffel bag in each hand like toolboxes. With a serious expression on his face, he moved decisively across the room and greeted us with a slight nod. Then he plonked the bags on the bed, tucked his hand into the outer pockets of one of them, and retrieved a pair of purple surgical gloves. He unfurled the right glove and fed his fingers through it before tugging at the base until the elasticity of the latex snapped it back to his wrist. He did the same with the other glove. When he was done, he interlocked his fingers in a satisfied clasp.

"Edward, right?" he asked, cross-checking.

"Yes, um, doctor?" I inquired.

"McDonald, Dr. McDonald," he said with a modest smile, as if to ease my nerves.

I figured from how sunken his face looked that he must've been one of those chronically exhausted doctors with an unflinching dedication to serving communities at the coalface of healthcare—to whom the NHS probably owed a debt of gratitude for suturing the fractures in the system with his commitment. Despite his apparent fatigue, Dr. McDonald exuded a calm confidence that momentarily put me at ease.

He meandered over to me and began carrying out his home-based consultation. "So you've called me in for severe cramping due to constipation?"

I nodded tensely, hoping for a quick and easy solution.

"May I?" Dr. McDonald asked, rolling up my sweater to reveal my belly. As he poked and prodded around my abdomen, I searched his face for any additional insight into the seriousness of my condition, but his expressions remained neutral.

"Your stomach is definitely distended. There's a lot in there," he said, confirming what I already knew. "I am going to insert a suppository into your anus, which should provide you relief within about half an hour."

A surge of disquietude washed over me. The notion of an audience watching as something was inserted up my derrière caught me off guard. Nevertheless, a suppository seemed like the obvious prescription to restore my insides to their former glory. Still, the anxiety of the mortifying choreography awaiting me canceled out any burgeoning relief I might have otherwise felt. Summoning all my courage, I took a deep breath and prepared myself for the next leg of the examination. *Ugh, here goes nothing,* I thought.

Surveying the room, my gaze settled on Four and Five, who seemed to have melded with the wall behind them. They avoided meeting my eyes, as if wishing that they could simply vanish into Four's adjoining room. Dr. McDonald caught me side-eyeing and asked, with a hint of skepticism, "I'm assuming those are your care aides?" I nodded in reluctant affirmation, sensing his unspoken reservation about them: *they don't inspire confidence.*

"Can you both help me get him onto the bed so we can get this young man some treatment?" Dr. McDonald asked.

Four and Five exchanged uncertain gestures, each looking to the other to take the lead. I rolled my eyes while they hesitated.

I don't want to be here any more than you guys, I thought. I'd much rather be at Turtle Bay with my friends, relishing in their company, than being the ball of this ping-pong match.

Four caved first. "I'll get the hoist," she said. She vanished into the bathroom and, in a few seconds, emerged with the crane, rolling it over to me. Five stepped forward, snatching the sling, which sat on top of the crane in a heap. I bent forward, allowing him to tuck the sling behind and under me. With the enthusiasm of a potted plant, he fed the straps between my thighs.

"Thanks so much for doing this," I said, hoping to disarm him with gratitude and charm, as if they were currency in exchange for compassion and patience. Five gave me a curt nod and signaled Four to lower the hoist. The hoist began its gradual ascent, lifting me up from my seat until I was suspended in the air, face-to-face with Dr. McDonald. I muscled up a nervous smile, feeling vulnerable and exposed in the elevated position. He tried hard to maintain his neutral expression, but behind the mask I could still identify the pity tracing the creases in the corners of his mouth.

With a slow and deliberate pace, Four lowered me back down to the bed, allowing Five to carefully remove my restraints. Then he rolled me onto my side holding me steady to prevent me from rolling back. As I lay there, my face pressed against the coarse fabric of his jeans, I detected the stench of mildew mixed with old food. Without warning, I felt my pants being pulled down. "Okay, Ed, just breathe," echoed Dr. McDonald's voice from behind me. I pinched my eyes shut and held my breath, defying the instruction. "You're doing really well, Ed," the doctor said as he inserted the suppository.

"And...you're all set!" he announced.

"Great job, Ed, great job," the physician said repeatedly as Five slackened his grip and plopped me down on my back.

"I suggest you sit him on the loo right away," the doctor advised Four and Five as I lay there on the bed panting. "By the time you guys are done strapping him into that thing, he will've already soiled himself." Dr. McDonald removed his gloves and tossed them into the wastebasket on the floor near the bed before leaning down to speak to me. Our noses were only a few inches apart. "Best of luck, lad. You're a brave man," he said, patting me gently on my chest.

As soon as Dr. McDonald left, I felt an immediate urge to use the bathroom. But that wasn't the first time I'd experienced a desperate need to go myself.

One day while at boarding school, I must have forgotten to watch my intake of orange juice during lunch as my bladder was on the verge of bursting. I was so afraid of accidentally wetting myself that I kept my hands in my lap, wiggled my bum, and shimmied to no beat in particular. I didn't know how much longer I could hold out, but I knew that it couldn't be much longer. Plus I had two hours of French with Madame G, whose patience, while generous, also had its limits.

I swiveled my neck and fixed my gaze on Laeticia, who was tidying the dishes after the lunch rush. Laeticia was the darling of the cafeteria. A cook with big brown eyes, an infectious laugh, and a disposition sweeter than M&Ms, she was everyone's favorite. We referred to her as Sis Laeticia. The "Sis" denoted endearment. And she referred to me as Mr. Ndopu. On this particular occasion, she called out my name and shuffled toward me, dancing in step with me, thinking that I was being silly and didn't want to go to class. "Everything okay, my dear?" she inquired.

Under normal circumstances, I'd have flashed an unassuming grin and said, *Yes, absolutely, just groovin' by myself.* But the pressure on my bladder had reached a critical level, and I was also aware that if I did pee on myself, I would have to sit in my soaked pants for four hours before Jackson, my care aide at the time, reported for duty.

So I threw away all my decorum and restraint and said, "Sis Laeticia, I need to ask you something. Ntate Jackson isn't here and I desperately need to pee. Do you think you could help me?"

I fully expected her to say no, after which I would've let it rip right there on the floor in front of her, making peace with the fact that I'd be scarred for life from the embarrassment.

But Sis Leticia surprised me and said, "Certainly, my dear, anytime." Her gold tooth glinted as she smiled. My doubts lingered, unsure if she truly grasped the intricacy of the task at hand and the vulnerability involved in aiding me with such a private matter. But I chose to place my trust in her, remembering the extra peanut butter and jelly sandwiches she would sneak on my tray every so often. If we were to see this through, we would have to face it together despite the awkwardness and embarrassment.

"Let's head to the bathroom. I'll show you what to do," I said. She led me into the stall, and I spent less than a minute running through the steps that comprised my peeing. She listened attentively but seemed to mirror the urgency I felt, as if she were experiencing the pressure I felt in my groin firsthand. She pulled me forward in my chair till I teetered at the edge. With one hand, she unzipped my pants while the other held the portable receptacle that I carried with me in my backpack. I winced. The most uncomfortable part was always a new hand inside my pants, the handling of my intimates. But it was also the line that helped me distinguish between the true empaths and the thoughts-and-prayers folk. Laeticia belonged to the former group as she did this unflinchingly, holding my genitalia over the open mouth of the receptacle. She wasn't in the let-us-know-if-you-need-anything crowd, where "anything" means nothing at all.

I held my breath, anticipating her reaction when I finished, expecting a look of regret, disgust, or something in between, but it never came. She disposed of the urine in the toilet, zipped me up, washed her hands, and carefully placed me at the right place on my chair. "Okay, Mr. Ndopu, you're all set. Now let's stop dancing and go to class," she joked, chuckling. This moment with Laeticia remains etched in my memory as a testament to what genuine care conveyed through deep empathy could truly look like. I can't recall if I ever expressed my gratitude—she wouldn't have let me anyway. Through her actions, Sis Laeticia instilled in me that I shouldn't have to feel excessively grateful for the kindness of others or be at their mercy when they are tasked with my care.

And so now as I was dangling butt naked from the crane, I

recognized the look of restrained disgust etched on Four's and Five's faces. I couldn't help but feel shame in response. "I'm so sorry, guys," I said. I didn't quite know what for. I just knew I was sorry—sorry things had to be this difficult.

Four and Five hoisted me down onto the toilet seat, and the solid thud of the bathroom door closing behind them was a relief in itself. It was a rare moment of solitude amid the clamor of my care routine. A euphoric release that can only be described as divine coursed through me. As my body purged itself of its afflictions, I marveled at the raw reality of my body: its fragilities, discomforts, spillages, and unruliness. With this acceptance came the understanding that the only way I would get through my graduate studies was if I leaned fully into what scared me tremendously: relinquishing the little control I had, asking for help, and allowing my body to exist in its own unapologetic way.

But first, there was the matter of my ballooning care costs. It was the biggest blockage of all, a daunting challenge that loomed over me. But as the colors around me seemed to intensify, the edges of the room sharpening back into focus, I felt my capacity for action and creativity return. I was ready for a do-over, ready to reclaim my agency. And I knew exactly what to do.

TEN

AS I AWAITED MY SUMMONS to what might very well prove to be the pivotal meeting of my academic tenure, I surveyed the sterile surroundings of the lobby in which I found myself seated. The barren atmosphere, with its uninspired IKEA furnishings and harsh, overhead halogen lights resembling twisted roots, offered little comfort. My gaze drifted to the clock on the wall, its hands silently marking the time as 8:35 a.m. I had been scheduled to meet with Oxford's upper echelon at 8:30 to address the financial quagmire that had befallen me since receiving the shocking email from the care agency three weeks prior.

I was eager to return to my studies, particularly the forthcoming lecture on the intricate relationship between human rights and public policy, the very reason I had pursued further education in the first place. As a driven individual with a passion for bettering the lives of the disabled community, I understood the importance of delving into the inner workings of government, lawmaking, and public administration in order to effect change. However, securing the £66,000 required to cover my care for the duration of my studies outweighed all other considerations. With determination in my heart, I resolved to remain in that lobby until a solution to my dire financial predicament was found. The university's willingness to meet with me at this juncture was heartening and seemed to indicate that they were finally taking my situation with the gravity it deserved.

I badly wanted to steal a peek inside the office where the various reps were currently locked in a premeeting, presumably to get on the same page about my predicament. So instead of doing the sensible thing and waiting there in the hallway compliantly, I let my inquisitiveness get the better of me. Lightly tapping the knob of my joystick, I moved stealthily, tiptoeing my wheelchair toward the door. Something creaked as my wheels rotated over the grooves carved into the hardwood floors, so I halted my movements, waited a second or two to establish that I was in the clear, and then inched myself forward again. I wheeled up close enough to the door to see through the vertical glass panel next to it, but not so close to the entryway that I'd alert those behind it to my not-so-subtle attempt to eavesdrop.

In a grand boardroom, adorned with luxurious furnishings,

a group of individuals attired in misfitting suits gathered around a grandiose table. Some of them were engrossed in mirthful laughter, while others nodded vehemently. Observing their jovial demeanor, I felt like a curious child studying the mood of their parent in hopes of finding the perfect moment to request a treat. At the head of the table stood *The Director*, a familiar face to me, whom I had encountered on several occasions. Known for her exceptional talent for transforming any interaction into a strategic opportunity, she was a professional power player, well-attuned to the status in the room. Her plain and unassuming appearance, consisting of unkempt brunette hair, a bare face, and gender-neutral attire, spoke volumes of women of her generation, who now held the reins of power and believed that a plain appearance was crucial to commanding respect. On this particular day, *The Director's* attire was a shapeless navy suit, which added to her already modest appearance. As our eyes met, I found myself unable to look away and mustered a smile, pretending it was intentional. She greeted me with a gesture of recognition, and opening the door just a crack, she flashed a smile and said, "Eddie, we'll be with you shortly." Embarrassed to have been caught in my scrutiny, I quickly retreated to my parking spot.

This time I remained put. *Everything's going to be just fine,* I tried to convince myself. Beneath my pensiveness was something akin to defiance. I figured that there was no way the Oxford executives I was about to meet with would sit back and watch me go down in flames halfway through the semester.

131

They'd surely want to see me thrive. After all, it wasn't the first time I was counting on higher-ups to help me leave a meeting certain of my future.

Years earlier, at eighteen years old, I found myself sitting at a mahogany boardroom table on the fiftieth floor of the plush headquarters of an African logistics conglomerate in the heart of Johannesburg's central business district. I was about to meet with the CEO and his top brass to persuade them to fund my undergraduate studies. First semester's tuition was due in three days, and I had no plan B.

Mom was a nervous wreck sitting next to me and tightly holding my hand as we silently waited for the high-level delegation to join us in the boardroom. We were accompanied by our family friend, Auntie Winnie, who'd made the meeting possible through a childhood friend of hers. Though more relaxed than Mom, she too feared for me. It wasn't long before I heard a warm, booming voice calling my name from behind. Mom and Auntie Winnie rose from their seats in synchrony. A distinguished-looking man with a full head of white hair suddenly appeared in the corner of my eye. He meandered into the palatial setting, stood across from me, and rested his hands on the table. Two men in well-fitting designer suits trailed behind him.

"Deeply honored to meet you, young man." He sat down, and like dominoes falling in staggered fashion, everyone else followed suit. "My team and I are huge fans of yours, Eddie. We are so delighted to have the opportunity to get to know you better. Congratulations on all you have accomplished. I still can't believe you are only eighteen years old and already going to college. It's truly remarkable." He turned to Mom, who by this time was fighting back tears. "You must be so proud. You've raised Africa's very own Stephen Hawking." Mom smiled modestly and murmured a thank-you, trying— but actually failing—to keep it together.

Then he asked me to tell him about myself and what I hoped to accomplish through my studies in Canada. Realizing that I would never get an opportunity like this again, I channeled the activist in me and waxed lyrical about how I intended to use my degree to deepen my advocacy with respect to fighting for the human rights of disabled people around the world.

Suddenly, I saw the eyes around the table enlarge. The CEO himself turned pale, as if he had seen something unsightly. Did I say something wrong? Did I blow it? Panicked, I kept a poker face. Seconds later, I felt a hand from behind squeeze my shoulder. I swiveled my head, looked down, and saw the hand of an elderly man. The entire room rose from their seats and stood to attention. One of the well-dressed men sitting next to the CEO gasped and let out an involuntary "Wow." The hand moved away, and I rotated my head further to catch a better glimpse of the presence that had just engulfed the room.

He looked like a cricket umpire in his tan chinos, navy blue blazer, polo shirt, and panama hat. He walked toward the CEO with his hand stretched out. It was Pius Langa, the retired chief justice of the Constitutional Court of South Africa. A bona fide national treasure. Nelson Mandela had personally appointed Langa to lead the highest court in the land following the end of apartheid—and he had just gate-crashed my meeting.

"Mr. Chief Justice, it's an honor, sir," the CEO said, over-whelmed and confused.

"Sorry I'm late," he said. I turned to Auntie Winnie, the only calm person in the room, surveying her demeanor for subtle clues. She winked at me. I later found out that she was introduced to Langa at church of all places. It was genius.

Of course, I got the money. I might have been fine on my own. The CEO might have agreed to fund my education of his own accord—but he couldn't deny me in front of Pius Langa. The stakes were too high to leave it up to chance.

Now my chances felt more slim than ever from the dizzy-ing heights of the number one ranked university in the world. "Eddie, please come through," *The Director* said, swinging the door open. I wheeled myself inside, and *The Director* motioned for me to park myself in the space that had presumably been created for my wheelchair. I heard her shut the door behind me as the participants took their seats. After taking her own seat, *The Director* swayed from side to side in her swivel chair across from me. She leaned forward and placed her hands on the table in an interlocked clasp to kick off the meeting. "Eddie, thank you for trusting us with this. We're sorry to hear about your recent financial setbacks. But I think we may have landed on a solution for you that'll help eliminate that burden..."

I smiled, almost unconsciously, as the words spilled out of her mouth. Finally, I was on track to reclaiming my Oxford experience. While I wished the university had stepped in earlier to bolster my scholarship, reflecting the true cost of my admission, I couldn't have been happier that they seemed to be doing so now. Of course, as I sat there overcome with relief and joy, I knew that the additional financial support I was anticipating would only win me half the battle. There was still the question of how to fix the revolving door of hopelessly disappointing care aides assigned to my case. But with the crushing weight of the funding shortfall lifted I would have additional bandwidth to come up with a plan to secure my care for the remaining nine months of the program.

As I leaned forward, eager for *The Director's* proposal, I envisioned the unlocking of some discretionary funding. "Eddie," she began, her tone filled with excitement. "Last week, I had the pleasure of speaking with the provost. And I am delighted to inform you that the university is willing to extend a most unusual offer. You will have the chance to complete your degree from the comfort of your home in South Africa, with the help of Skype. This will eliminate the cost of care altogether. Is this not wonderful news?"

The words struck me like a thunderbolt. Was she serious? I cast a quick gaze around the room, studying the faces of the bureaucrats seated beside her. Their nods confirmed what my ears had heard. I was at a loss for words, a grin frozen on my face, as I attempted to process this unexpected turn of events. How could the cessation of my active academic life be considered "wonderful news?" Was this a covert method for them to ask me to drop out? A way for the university to shirk its responsibility toward disabled students like myself? The thought filled me with anger. I refused to be shortchanged after all the struggles I had overcome to reach this point. I clenched my jaw and met *The Director's* gaze, determined to fight for what I deserved.

Inhaling deeply, I summoned all my diplomacy: "Allow me to express my gratitude for your attempts to resolve what is undoubtedly a challenging predicament. However, if I understand correctly, this degree has been promoted as a professional, hands-on program that brings together ambitious young leaders from across the globe to be trained in working across cultures and disciplines with the aim of becoming more proficient practitioners of public policy. Is this not so?" I couldn't help but observe one of the representatives fidgeting, as if to silently concede my point. "Therefore, I must confess my confusion as to how you believe this program's ethos and purpose could be fulfilled through remote participation."

The Director leaned back in her chair, a sign of her surprise at my response, and stroked her chin pensively. "You raise a valid argument," she said, her tone measured. "It is not our preference for you to leave the campus, and we appreciate your desire for the full Oxford experience. However, given the circumstances, this may be the most viable solution. Rest assured: we will make every effort to ensure that you do not feel isolated."

This is utter nonsense, I thought. The reasoning was full of flaws. "Excuse me, does this mean that the university is unable to provide financial support or adjust my scholarship?" I asked, redirecting the conversation toward what I believed was a more practical solution.

"Pardon me," interjected one of the representatives, his tone as monotonous as his bland attire. "From the college's standpoint, Eddie, we would like to offer our assistance. However, Somerville's budget is limited in comparison to larger colleges. Regrettably, our hands are somewhat tied." His measured speech betrayed a sense of unease, as if he were grappling with this difficult conversation as much as I was. "As I understand it, just as you bear the responsibility for your living expenses, so too you bear the responsibility for the cost of your care, as it is considered a private matter." I couldn't help but question the accuracy of this statement, as my scholarship included a living allowance and funds for room and board. He continued: "With the inclusion of the costs for the two rooms occupied by your caretakers, the total endowment for the year comes to £80,000. This is a substantial sum, even higher than your initial estimate, and we wouldn't want to set an unreasonable precedent."

I felt a heavy weight press against my chest, uncertain whether it was my heart or some other vital organ. I was on

137

the brink of tears, but I couldn't let them see me break down. To do so would only reinforce their determination to send me away.

"Eighty thousand pounds?" I repeated, trying to hide my shock behind a blank expression. No one dared to utter the obscene amount, as if doing so would only magnify the absurdity of the situation. A stalemate had been reached. "I need to weigh my options and think this through before making a decision," I said.

The Director chimed in, "Of course, of course, take all the time you need. We are here for you, whatever you decide." Her words, however, rang hollow, lacking genuine compassion and sounding more like a formality. I was truly on my own.

She glanced at her watch and, to my surprise, the meeting had not only ended on time but had been much shorter than I had anticipated. She rose from her seat and declared, "Thank you for coming, Eddie." As she led me to the door, I politely thanked everyone for their time and informed them I would be in touch after careful consideration. I then turned and swiftly made my exit.

As I rounded the corner, a deep sigh escaped my lips, the aftershocks of what felt like an ambush still rippling through my being. *What the fuck was that?* I wondered. But I knew that there was no time for rumination, for class was about to begin, and I needed to present a composed front.

I hastened down the corridor, propelling my wheelchair

toward the elevators. Just in the nick of time, someone emerged, allowing me to slip into the elevator. Being alone and in need of assistance with doors or elevators often meant I was left waiting for a passerby to come to my aid.

"Hold the door, ma'am!" I called out to the woman, who I assumed was one of the many faceless bureaucratic employees who rarely ventured out of their cubicles to interact with us students. "What floor?" she asked as I rushed in. "Ground floor, please," I replied.

As I descended, I pondered the implications of the university's recent proposal to complete my degree via Skype. If I were to succumb, I thought, the logistics would be a nightmare. How could I manage around-the-clock support for my needs, especially with my mother growing older? The idea was not nearly as practical as it might have seemed.

With newfound resolve, I disembarked from the elevator and made my way to the auditorium where my lecture on project management was about to begin. As a disabled young Black person, I felt a moral obligation to complete my degree in person at Oxford, not from an apartment in Johannesburg with spotty Wi-Fi. I was determined to find a better solution.

I entered the auditorium with burgeoning passion and took my designated seat, overlooking the cascading rows of seats leading down to the podium. My professor, a typical absent-minded philosopher, was at the bottom getting ready for the lecture, while my classmates milled about, chatting and laughing. My university-appointed notetaker, Judy, was already seated next to me, fully immersed in the day's reading and eager to participate in the class discussions.

Just moments before the lecture was about to begin, a group of my classmates congregated at my desk. Ade, the charismatic Nigerian student who saw himself as the next Steve Jobs, said, "We would like you to run for the position of student body president, Eddie."

Me? I thought. I had been able to keep my personal struggles separate from my academic performance, participating fully in class and impressing my peers and professors. To my excited peers, I must have looked like I had my shit together—making thoughtful interventions in class, making it to parties off campus, and smiling all the way through. I could already see the headlines blazed across Cherwell, Oxford's student-run newspaper: "Blavatnik School Elects Its First Disabled African Student Body President."

With this in mind, I considered the suggestion to run for student body president. But with recent developments, my ability to maintain that balance was becoming increasingly difficult. I needed to find a way to demonstrate my value to the university and secure my place in Oxford to continue my studies. But this was a weighty decision that required further thought and consultation with my trusted inner circle. If I had developed the courage to open up to Oxford's administration, then surely it was time to open up to my squad.

"Let me think about it," I said to my classmates turned would-be constituents.

Sipping Dom Pérignon Through a Straw

"Okay, don't think too long," Priscilla, from Zimbabwe, said. "We've already started canvassing for you."

IT WAS LATER THAT AFTERNOON during a communal feast in my dorm, where the squad had gathered, that I revealed the truth of my recent struggles. We settled ourselves on the floor and bed, surrounding plates overflowing with savory delights of jollof rice, succulent peanut chicken stew, crispy fried plantain, and soft dumplings.

As we ate, I unburdened myself, speaking of the university's request for me to complete my degree via remote learning. Auntie Viv was taken aback, nearly choking on a piece of bone marrow.

My friends were shocked and outraged, voicing their support for me. "That's unacceptable," Aïda exclaimed. "You deserve to be here in person, just like the rest of us. They were well aware of your talents and your disability when they offered you admission," she exclaimed, spooning jollof rice into my mouth. "And now they want to cast you aside, as if your genius and influence as a disabled person don't contribute to their reputation and financial success." She shook her head in disapproval.

Jess placed a comforting hand on my shoulder. "I can't imagine how difficult this must be for you," she said softly. "You're more than capable of completing your degree on campus."

But amid the outpouring of support, Tebs seemed hesitant, citing the obvious concern about funding. "I understand why you would want to stay, but think about the financial implications," he said. "It might not be possible for you to strong-arm the school into supporting you."

Jess was quick to push back, however, her eyes blazing with determination. "We can't let funding be the reason why he has to leave," she declared. "He's breaking barriers by being here, and we can't let that go to waste."

I looked around at my friends, feeling a sense of comfort wash over me. No matter what, they had my back and I felt validated in my fight for my right to complete my degree on campus.

Feeling comfortable enough to be vulnerable, I decided to take the squad into my confidence and told them about the kind of care I was receiving. I was reminded of a recent disappointment, having asked for Five to be removed from my care after he lectured me on the evils of my sexuality. It started off as an innocuous conversation. We were talking about his family when he made a casual comment about how much he disliked queer folks. In that moment, I realized with a sinking feeling that he was homophobic. I wasn't entirely sure how to react. I was torn between my surprise and my shock.

As I sat there, I found that I could no longer look at Five the same way. I had trusted him, and to hear him express such sentiments was heartbreaking. This was someone who was supposed to be taking care of me, someone who was supposed to be a model of acceptance and understanding. It was an awful realization.

I opened my mouth to say something, but before I could even begin, Five had changed the subject. I knew that he could tell I was upset, but he made no effort to apologize or explain his comments. I was once again facing another disappointment, another complaint, and another heartbreak. My financial constraints left me with no choice but to remain with my current agency.

Jess nodded sympathetically, adding, "And the care you're receiving is inadequate. It's absurd that you had to ask me to cut your nails the other day. According to the agency, that requires a professional and added fees."

The squad's expressions were filled with concern and uncertainty. "Here's hoping your new caretaker is better," said Jess. Indeed, I could only hope for improvement.

ELEVEN

THANKS FOR WHEELING HIM OUT," the facilities manager said to Six, one upright to another. He didn't even
acknowledge my existence as I sat there outside in the concourse on the morning of the fire drill, virtually naked,
quivering under the pitiful towel Six had draped over me
just before yanking me out of the shower. Six, on the other
hand, looked pleased with himself, like an underling who'd
just received props from the big boss for a job well done. I
was incensed but outwardly calm. I'd already decided that I
was going to have him fired before close of business that day.
"Right. We're in the clear. Off you go to your rooms," the
facilities manager barked, flailing his hands as he motioned
for everyone gathered there in the courtyard to get a move on.

When I returned to my dorm, I didn't bother hopping back

into the shower for fear of wasting more time. I had Six get me dressed for the electoral process that was scheduled to commence within the hour. I'd wound up settling for the easiest outfit that I could be dressed in. It also happened to be the most drab—a gray-and-black Nike sweatsuit that had lost all its color from reckless overwashing. Not exactly presidential attire, but if it meant getting out of the door faster, it had to do. I also skipped breakfast entirely, helping me recoup some of the time that had been stolen from me.

Breathless and still somewhat shaken from the harrowing ordeal Six had put me through, I was able to wheel myself into the auditorium around 8:45 a.m. Some of my classmates had trickled into the room, coffees in hand, but most of them still dawdled outside. It seemed I had about ten or so minutes to kill before the rest of the student body would have to endure listening to each candidate make their case for being elected student body president. After that, we would all be required to cast our ballots in the foyer. Ever bright-eyed and bushy-tailed, my notetaker, Judy, was already there, fingers poised over her laptop as she sat next to me. In that moment, I envied her bottomless capacity to be enamored by student life. "Hey, could you please help me draft an email?" I asked her somewhat sheepishly. I'd figured I'd use the extra time miraculously afforded to me to quickly dictate an email of complaint to the care agency, demanding they send me someone new.

"Sure," Judy replied. As I detailed the horrors of the fire drill incident, my voice wobbled and Judy's otherwise lively fingers slackened. She turned to me, her eyes the size of marbles, and whispered, "That really happened?" I nodded. And before I knew it the emotion in me had surged up to the brim and overflowed. "Oh, Eddie, I am so sorry," she said, as she stood up and hugged me.

"Everyone will be here soon. Best we clean that email up and send it through," I said, shoving the tears back inside me to restore my composure. Right after we sent the email I filed the entire incident away in the same place as my tears and channeled my energy toward my presidential bid and what I was going to say to win it. I was woefully underprepared, having spent all of my free time going back and forth with the administration and sinking further into stress and anxiety. Thankfully, my supporters—all Black students from various parts of the world—had rallied to set me up for an Obama moment. My natural propensity for public speaking to large crowds would have to carry me through this last phase.

It was just after nine o'clock. The auditorium was filled with students and even some administrators and staff. The guy I was up against slunk into the room, somehow later to the function than me, dressed to kill in a charcoal suit. He had all the hallmarks of a formal leader. He was tall, conventionally attractive, neither adored nor disliked, serious, but not too bland. Basically, the quintessential upright in every sense imaginable. And as he took to the podium and began presenting his platform, it became clear that this was the ticket on which he was running. "While I think Eddie is incredibly inspirational, this role requires more than inspiration. As the student body, we need a president who can actually do this job. Someone with obvious leadership skills and a demonstrable track record of getting stuff done. I am that person." Every now and then heads would swivel to take inventory of my reaction to what was being said. From his tone of speech to the way he latched on to the podium, as if to devour it, he truly believed he had it in the bag. Several of my classmates nodded along in agreement as he spoke. I sat in the back, my smile glued to my face because I didn't want to be caught with an inferable face. *If you think you're going to win this thing by appealing to subconscious bias, you are going to have to try harder, buddy. You've taken on the wrong crip.*

Finally, after his ableist mudslinging, it was my turn to take the floor. I wheeled myself down the ramp that wound up to the front of the auditorium. Because the podium was too high for me to be seen from behind it, my Venezuelan classmate had offered to sit beside me and direct a handheld mic to my mouth as I presented my vision. Lord only knew why there was no lapel mic, but this ended up working out to my advantage as it gave me an entry point to make a larger point. I decided on the spot to throw out my prepared remarks and speak off the cuff instead. "Let's address the elephant in the room," I began. "I may need someone to hold the mic for me, but I am more than capable of amplifying your voice as students." Once the words leapt from my mouth I was off to the races. It was what one might have called *a mic drop moment*. The room erupted in applause as soon as I'd finished.

Afterward, upon casting our ballots, one of my Australian classmates came up to me and said, "You should feel really good about yourself. That was sensational." Something about the warmth in her face, the care of her smile, disarmed me and made me open up and tell her how I'd really felt.

"I'm scared," I said, probably the truest thing I'd said all day. The angelic expression on her face collapsed into a concerned frown. "I don't quite know how to say this. But if I win, it means I can't make one wrong move because if I do it will be attributed to my disability. People will say, 'We should have known this role was going to be too difficult for someone like him.' I don't know, maybe I'm overthinking things, but I'm scared that I might not live up to the pressure I've created for myself." Worried that I just might have revealed too much, I brightened up my face with a smile, putting my mask back on.

My Australian classmate shook her head. "I think you're definitely overthinking this. You're going to make a wonderful president." She was firm in her conviction, but the knot in my stomach tightened still. The truth was, my feeling of failure was because of the financial crisis I had been plunged into.

"Let's hope so," I said.

TWELVE

EDDIE, PLEASE, COME IN," *The Director* said, summoning me inside her corner office as she held the door open for me to enter. Her deputy, a middle-aged man with a slicked-back hairdo who always seemed to find a way to weave his Scottish patriotism into every conversation, even if it was about something mundanely unrelated, like traffic, was draped over the chair at the table adjacent to her desk. While I was maneuvering myself into position across from him, he greeted me with a slight nod of the head. I reciprocated with a mouthed hello. "So, first things first," *The Director* said as she plonked herself down in the seat next to him. "Massive congratulations on your election, Eddie! I heard through the grapevine that you delivered a cracker of a speech and won last week. Good for you."

"Thanks. I'm looking forward to advocating for our collective interests as students," I said, pressing my lips together in a corporate smile. I could tell from the artificial grin on her face that she'd expected less of a protocol-tinged response. But the advocate in me couldn't resist the opportunity to, well, advocate.

"Wonderful," she said, somewhat disinterestedly. "Anyway, Eddie, I called you in today because it's been a few weeks since our last meeting. It's clear from how deeply immersed you are in student life—which we *love* to see—that you have every intention of staying on campus. We therefore propose that you consider a crowdfunding campaign."

"A crowdfunding campaign?" I asked, somewhat rhetorically.

"Yes, they're known to be incredibly successful. Last year we had a student who fell ill unexpectedly and was eventually hospitalized. Her healthcare costs quickly ballooned. She found herself unable to pay her bills, so she started a fundraising campaign. And the outpouring of support was so lovely to see. I think this might be your best bet."

Have you forgotten? I thought. *I've been down this road before with #OxfordEddiecated.* Because I was intimately familiar with just how intensive and laborious mounting a crowdfunding campaign truly was, I resented how flippantly she'd just invoked the idea, as though it was a piece of cake. What's more, my situation couldn't be compared to someone raising money for a medical procedure. She still didn't get it. I should never have been required to fundraise for an accommodation

152

that ought to have been provided without qualification in the first place. But because I had wanted this opportunity more than I'd wanted anything else, I did what I had to do to get in. And now because I'd been backed into a corner, I essentially had to do what was being asked of me in order to stay. Dropping out of the program was not an option, even though I wasn't at all sure if I had enough in me to manage another crowdfunding campaign alongside a full course load and my new duties as student body president. But once again seated in front of a wall of bureaucracy, what choice did I have? "Um, yeah...I guess I could do that. I mean, as you know, I already did—"

"So then this shouldn't be too difficult for you," *The Deputy* interrupted, smiling maniacally. "We'll be rooting for you."

Seconding him, *The Director* chirped, "Absolutely." Then she straightened her posture and said, "Look, Eddie, I am afraid I must get ready for my next meeting. But we also were thinking that it might be a good idea to disclose your situation to your classmates. They may be able to help."

Hmmm, that sounds like a conflict of interest, I thought. Something about it also felt icky. I didn't want anyone to pity me, especially my classmates. But before I could voice my discomfort, *The Director* instructed her deputy to accompany me right there and then to my statistics class, where I'd be given the first few minutes before the lecture was going to begin to disclose my plight. This felt nonconsensual, no different from when Six yanked me out of the shower and paraded me naked outside in front of my college mates. Though I was fully clothed now, I still felt stripped bare, right down to my insides.

The Deputy led the way as I wheeled into the auditorium.

The squad, seated together toward the back rows, shrugged their shoulders in puzzled curiosity as I drove past the space that had been reserved for my wheelchair and down to the front of the hall.

"Can I get everyone's attention?" *The Deputy* announced, nipping the chatter in the bud. "I'd like to invite Eddie to step forward to address you all today in a personal capacity." He gestured for me to take the floor. I flicked my joystick forward and positioned myself next to the podium. As I cast my eyes out onto the auditorium at all the faces that stared back down at me, it dawned on me that every region of the world was represented in the room. This only served to heighten my anxiety. I felt as if I'd just been asked to engage in high-stakes diplomacy at the United Nations, a dream I'd harbored for as long as I could remember, but if it was anything like this, I'd have to pass. This was not the way I'd hoped to kick off my term as president, accidentally personifying the stereotype of the begging, pleading disabled African that my opponent had seeded in their minds.

There I sat in the lowest, yet most visible place in the room, being asked to make a hundred people see what ten higher-ups couldn't.

I exhaled sharply and began articulating, as honestly as

Sipping Dom Pérignon Through a Straw

I knew how, what it was like carrying an eighty-thousand-pound load on my back. I chose not to disclose the other dimension of my lived experience—the neglect, the constipation, the humiliation—because frankly what I needed more than anything was support, not pity or pushback. I thought I could address them while still showing grit and resilience. As their student body president, the last thing I wanted was for them to see a chip in my makeshift armor.

But then my voice cracked.

No amount of grit could stop the tears that oozed out of me. I was furious at my body for its physiological response. It felt like a flagrant betrayal of my promise to myself to maintain my dignity, even when my back was against the wall, something I'd learned from Mom. It didn't make me feel any better when a handful of my classmates leaned forward and wiped away tears from their cheeks as I crumbled in front of them.

After I said my piece, I received scattered applause. If I'd been offered the option of evaporating into a plume of smoke, I'd have gladly taken it. But all I could do was back myself up against the whiteboard and try to make peace with the fact that I'd just outed myself as a desperately vulnerable person.

The Deputy squeezed my shoulder on his way back to the podium. "Thanks, Eddie, for sharing your plight with us. You are an inspiration to us all. Eddie will be creating a crowdfunding campaign. If any of you'd be so inclined as to make donations toward Eddie's cause, that would be greatly appreciated." I lowered my gaze to the floor, awash with feelings of condescension and shame. "Right, any questions before we move on?" he asked. Crickets. Then, just as *The Deputy* was about to switch gears, one of my classmates, an American from the Midwest, raised his hand.

"Don't get me wrong. I feel sorry for him," he said, as though I wasn't in the room. "But what if I had debt coming into Oxford? Shouldn't it be my responsibility?" Murmurings sparked throughout the room with some agreeing with him and others arguing out loud that he'd made a false equivalence. "Yeah, but how are we defining debt? Surely this is different?" my classmate from Azerbaijan said. To which someone else retorted, "Why? Because he's in a wheelchair?" A flaming debate raged on. I was now no longer a person but a real-time anthropological case study. My peers were more spirited than I'd seen them in front of any of our instructors, and yet they had no clue what I was actually going through behind closed doors. I sat there watching the gravity of my situation be reduced to a ping-pong match, each student trying to one-up the next. As for the squad, I could see from their stunned expressions that if they could they'd have whisked me out of there and spared me this humiliation.

"Why don't we continue this conversation after hours? It's time to move on," *The Deputy* said, wrangling the room. It was the first thing he said all day that was in my favor. I deeply needed to get out of there and clear my head, statistics be damned. As soon as *The Deputy* handed the room over to our professor, I wheeled myself out of the auditorium as fast as I could. I didn't look up at anyone as I sped toward the exit.

"Eddie, slow down," a voice called as I charged for the elevator. I swiveled 180 degrees. It was Zarifa, one of my classmates, a Yemeni student whom I had sometimes shared notes with. "Listen," she said, out of breath. "I know that couldn't have been easy. I'm really sorry. I think I know how we can solve this."

I stopped just short of the elevator doors. She'd piqued my curiosity. In my previous interactions with Zarifa, she had struck me as a deeply compassionate person, so in some ways, I felt like I could let my guard down and hear her out. I didn't have much else to lose at this point but my time.

"How's about I tell you all about it tomorrow over dinner and shisha? You ever had shisha?" she asked. I shook my head. Though I'd never smoked before, I was quite open to giving it a try. I was overdue for some fun. "You'll like it," she assured me. I'll swing by your dorm after six o'clock tomorrow and we'll go together. Let me get that for you." Zarifa reached past me, pressing the button to call the elevator down for me. As the doors closed, she gave a thumbs-up and jogged back to the auditorium.

THIRTEEN

ZARIFA AND I SET OUT on a leisurely stroll before our shisha-infused dinner date. We ambled past the charming storefronts that line Jericho Road, taking in the city with appreciative eyes. Oxford was a city transformed at night; the evening seemed to imbue it with a magical quality, as if granting us permission to shed our facades and reveal our true selves. The city was softer, more romantic, less hostile, and I couldn't help but bask in its beauty.

"Did you know that Stephen Hawking is speaking at the Oxford Union tonight?" Zarifa asked, her voice light as we passed the Oxford University Press building.

"Yeah, I heard about it. I really wanted to go, but tickets sold out in the first two hours. Apparently, people camped out in line all night just to get a chance to hear him speak,"

I replied. While theoretical physics was hardly my area of interest, Dr. Hawking's status as a profoundly disabled achiever adored by the masses and recognized for his genius reaffirmed my pursuit for an extraordinary life.

"They always have standing room. Wanna see if we can catch a glimpse of him before dinner?" she suggested.

"Sure, why not?" I responded, eager to see the renowned physicist in person.

We made our way to the Oxford Union, where Mr. Hawking was set to speak in just fifteen minutes. As I rolled down the cobblestone streets, I felt as if I were walking in the footsteps of giants. The air was electric with excitement, and I could feel the anticipation building within me with each rotation of my wheels. Zarifa was saying something, but her words were lost on me as I was lost in thought, contemplating the journey that had brought me to this moment.

The streets were packed with people, a throng of eager onlookers, all seeking a glimpse of the living legend. The lines snaked far into the distance, a testament to the reverence and awe that the citizens of this historic city held for Stephen Hawking. I was humbled by the sight of so many people who had braved the cold and damp just to hear him speak, camping out all night to secure a spot in line.

As we approached the Oxford Union, I felt a swelling of emotion. I had read about Stephen Hawking's incredible life and the relentless pursuit of knowledge he had undertaken despite his physical limitations.

Sipping Dom Pérignon Through a Straw

And then there he was, the man himself: Stephen Hawking in person. I made my way to the front of the crowd, exuding confidence and fooling security into believing that I had every right to be there.

As the black SUV pulled up slowly in front of the Oxford Union, I held my breath. Out came Stephen Hawking, his care assistant by his side. He descended the ramp with grace and fluidity, his movements a delicate dance between his body, his wheelchair, and his assistant. As he wheeled himself toward the entrance to the building, I positioned myself in his line of sight, eager for just a moment in his presence.

He wheeled himself right past me. *Stephen Hawking just wheeled himself right past me!!!* It was surreal.

I gazed upon Stephen Hawking in wonder and amazement while he navigated his chair with expert precision, his aura of intelligence and authority radiating outward. The sight of another disabled individual who had achieved so much filled me with pride. I was in the presence of a true visionary, a man who had dedicated his life to unlocking the mysteries of the universe. Standing there with Zarifa, I had my own Issa Rae moment: I'm rooting for everybody disabled.

Prof. Hawking's eyes met mine and, in that moment, I felt a deep connection to this remarkable man. I felt as if he were looking into my soul, understanding the struggles I faced and encouraging me to keep pushing forward. I was overcome with emotion, and I knew that this encounter would stay with me for the rest of my life.

As he drove his electric wheelchair into the Union, I felt a sense of longing. I wanted to follow him, to bask in the wisdom he was about to impart. But dinner called, and I had my own history to make. At least try.

As the chill of the evening set in, Zarifa and I hailed a taxi and made our way to the shisha lounge. Stepping inside, we were transported to a fashionable lounge in the heart of the Middle East. Button-tufted suede love seats were scattered about, amid Persian rugs and ornate lanterns, creating a tapestry of elegance and comfort.

The walls were adorned with plasma televisions that played hip-hop music videos, capturing the eclectic fusion of cultures that defined Oxford as a hub of cosmopolitanism. As we stood taking in our surroundings, a man in a dress shirt and tight jeans approached us, his chiseled pecs and sideburns exuding an air of ownership.

"*Habibti*," he greeted Zarifa, extending his arms warmly.

"Omar!" she cried out in elation, as if she had been reunited with a cherished friend after many years.

"Welcome back, my dear," Omar greeted her warmly, as they embraced in a tender hug. It was clear that Zarifa was a frequent visitor to this establishment. Omar turned to me, patted my shoulder, and said with a smile, "Nice to meet you, buddy." His accent, infused with the roughness of the cockney dialect, had an irresistible charm that elicited a grin from my lips. Before I could even respond, Omar rubbed his hands together and said, "Your table is ready. Follow me."

Sipping Dom Pérignon Through a Straw

We wound our way through the bustling floor, navigating between patrons seated around their billowing bowls of shisha. The smoke that rose from their lips and nostrils lingered in the air, as if clouds from the dreary sky had descended into the room.

In the midst of the fragrant fog, I detected hints of citrus and floral notes that saturated the air. Upon reaching our table, Zarifa gracefully slid into the wraparound booth built into the wall and beckoned me to join her. Omar moved a chair out of the way, creating a space for me to settle in. "I'll get you guys your shisha," he said, retiring the chair to the vacant side of the table. "What flavor are we going for tonight?"

Uncertain and feeling out of place, I looked to Zarifa for guidance. "We'll both have blackberry," she said, saving me from my inexperience.

"Excellent," Omar replied before promptly disappearing into the smoke-filled atmosphere.

Less than five minutes later, he returned, bearing a complex contraption and a pair of tongs in his hands. With gentle care, he placed the apparatus on the table. The bulb-like base was adorned with ropes that dangled from its sides, while a long rod, intricately decorated, sprouted from the top, fanning out to form a funnel, where the coals would be placed. From my perspective, the tiered structure looked like a chandelier that had come loose from its ceiling. Omar rummaged in his pocket, retrieving a foil packet. He unwrapped it with his teeth, revealing a mouthpiece that resembled that of a clarinet. He positioned it over the lip of one of the hanging hoses. With one hand, he held the hose, using the other to tend to the glowing, deep-orange coals that sat atop the bowl with the tongs. Once it was set up, he put the hose to his lips and inhaled deeply. An impressive cloud of smoke mushroomed from his mouth, eliciting a nod of satisfaction from him. "You guys are all set," Omar said, before switching the mouthpiece and extending the pipe toward me. "Take slow drags," he said with a tender smile.

This simple gesture moved me, notwithstanding the eyebrow-raising context. He'd figured out that I wasn't able to use my hands. And instead of being awkward about it, he'd taken it upon himself to offer up help without any fuss. I stared up at him with glazed eyes, cracked a smile, and then locked lips with the shisha hose, pulling in and releasing a pitiful puff into the air. I wasn't surprised. Considering how much weaker my lungs were to begin with, there was no way I'd have been able to produce clouds comparable to Omar's anyway. I probably shouldn't have been smoking in the first place, but hell, why not? Given how frequently we as disabled and chronically ill folks are placed in boxes marked "FRAGILE," this felt exhilaratingly revolutionary. Plus, it seemed to me that I should be allowed the chance to experiment with a vice at least once in my life. *"Live slightly dangerously,"* right?

Now it was Zarifa's turn, so she got herself set up with a mouthpiece on the other hose. Then we watched her show off her chops as the shisha queen she was. "Check this out," she said, as she inhaled a gulp and subsequently exhaled several perfectly shaped Os in quick succession. Omar and I chuckled in amazement.

"Be right back with your food," Omar said, as he laid my hose down on the table in front of Zarifa, presumably so she could take over and help me smoke whenever I needed. As we waited, I figured I'd get to the heart of why we were meeting up. "So, Zarifa, you said that you had an idea for how I might be able to solve my financial problems."

She wagged her finger and said, "First, tell me how you got into this mess."

For the next hour, while digging into the scrumptious food we had ordered, I took Zarifa into my confidence, recounting the backstory of how I had to source care from the UK and even fundraise for it despite the fact that Oxford had awarded me a scholarship. "I feel like I'm always fighting an uphill battle," I told her, my voice shaking with emotion. "From the lack of accessibility around campus to the ableism I face in my classes, it's like the university was built for able-bodied students only."

My friend listened intently, her eyes filled with empathy. She reached across the table and took my hand, offering me a comforting squeeze.

"I had no idea," she said softly. "I'm so sorry you have to go through this."

As I continued to pour my heart out, she nodded along, encouraging me to keep talking. Her unwavering support and understanding meant the world to me in that moment.

"This all sounds so unfair," Zarifa lamented, pausing to take another drag. "It's a story that needs to be told. So here's my idea: I used to work for Al Jazeera. I was on the phone earlier this week catching up with a former colleague, Neave, Neave Barker. He's a great reporter. If you're keen, I can get him to do a story about this."

As we wrapped up our meal and made our way back to our respective homes, relief washed over me. It was a feeling I had not experienced in a long time—to be understood, to be heard, and to have someone acknowledge the reality of the situation I was facing. My friend had leveraged her power as a compassionate listener—and former employee at a globally syndicated news outlet—to offer me solace at a time of need.

The streets were bathed in the warm glow of streetlamps, which cast a peaceful light on the cobblestone roads as we walked. I was in a daze, still processing the cathartic experience of finally sharing my struggles with someone who didn't diminish the truth of my experiences.

"Thank you," I said, breaking the silence between us. "It means so much to me that you're here for me and that you understand what I'm going through."

She smiled at me, her eyes shining with kindness. "Of course," she said. "That's what friends are for."

As we said our goodbyes and went our separate ways, I felt a newfound sense of hope. In a world where ableism and institutional neglect are all too real, Zarifa had offered me a small but powerful act of kindness that reminded me that I was not alone in this fight.

LATER THAT WEEK, ZARIFA'S FORMER colleague from Al Jazeera, Neave Barker, showed up at Oxford with a large film crew geared up for our week-long shoot. I was now ready to play ball. Having a global news organization on campus changed the terms of engagement. The media has power—so by extension I had power.

Oxford officials began to take me seriously now that my entourage included a camera crew. Members of the administration pulled me out of class more than once over the week and told me that this was a golden opportunity to solicit support for my cause. There was no room for negativity, they suggested repeatedly. It was easy to surmise that the administration was worried about how they would be perceived by the general public.

In preparation for filming for the feature, Al Jazeera had a makeup artist on standby to conceal the dark marks around my eyes that had formed from weeks of stress. But there was no concealer for the emotional bruising I felt from trying to hold on to what remained of my dreams. This—the feature, the thousands of people who would see it, even the money— was not about Oxford. It was about institutional life writ large.

It was my duty to tell the truth and nothing but—I needed to, and now more than ever, I wanted to.

The film crew followed me while I showed them what a day in my life looked like. I showed them the contraptions in my room: the hoist, the slings, the hospital bed with the guardrails surrounding it. I showed them how tricky it was to navigate the cobblestone streets in my wheelchair between classes. I even showed them the flight of stairs that barred me from using one of the cafeterias, extending my daily journey for meals by fifteen minutes both ways.

The Al Jazeera feature aired three weeks later on the news outlet's global prime-time bulletin. That night, a Friday, a bunch of us—the squad, Zarifa, and supporters from my campaign and various classes—gathered in my dorm room for a viewing party. I sat sandwiched between my friends and classmates as we huddled around a thirteen-inch MacBook Air perched on the edge of my desk, which we'd pushed up against the wall below the window. The night sky outside looked so clear, as if it had a sheen to it, like black patent leather. Zarifa heaved herself up from a beanbag and shuffled toward my laptop. She crouched down and fiddled with the mouse pad to begin streaming the live broadcast. As she buried her head in the screen, briefly obstructing our view, I exhaled sharply. Suddenly this all felt like an awful idea. I was careful in what I had said but truthful in my account of my time at Oxford so far. Still, I feared that my words would be taken out of context and infused with vengeance against the school that I had not expressed outright. "Tell me again why I agreed to do this," I said through a nervous chuckle to no one in particular. "I should have kept my mouth shut."

"And risk the possibility of being sent home? Not a chance! You did the right thing," Anika, one of the dozen Australians in our class, said, draping herself on the edge of my bed.

I nodded, unconvinced. Sensing my trepidation and anxiety, Tebs, seated in the chair next to me, hugged me sideways, his hands clasped together under my armpit as he gently laid his head against my shoulder.

"It's showtime," Zarifa said, crawling back to her spot and nestling herself in.

We watched a sports bulletin and the global weather forecast. Then the anchor announced my feature. Fatou, my classmate from Sierra Leone, squealed, and Zarifa hushed us all up. "Shhh, guys, let's listen up."

A close-up shot of my face filled the frame as I appeared to be lying on my back with my head elevated against a pillow. The camera then zoomed out to reveal my care aides strapping me into the sling, with each of them hunched over me on either side of the bed's guardrails.

As I was being hoisted up, Neave's voiceover began to contextualize the imagery unfolding before our eyes:

> Eddie Ndopu is one of the brightest minds at the world's leading university. He also needs constant care. He was diagnosed with Spinal Muscular Atrophy as an infant, and given only a few years to live.

As the segment cut to a medium shot of me delivering an into-the-camera confessional from the very spot I was sitting in now, I held my breath. *Oh God, I hope I didn't run my mouth too much*, I thought, using my lackluster strength to squeeze Tebs's hand.

> "I've developed an intimate relationship with discomfort. I think discomfort is part and parcel of what it means to survive and exist."

I let out an audible gasp as I watched myself articulate my experience with such philosophical depth and insight. I seemed to have taken a page from Greek mythology and adopted a Sisyphean worldview, sounding at peace with the notion of rolling a boulder up a mountain only for it to be sent back down so I could roll it back up again, repeating the process again and again and again and again. *You shouldn't have to be this strong,* I thought. I felt a hand squeeze my knee. Someone else whispered, "You've got this," as I continued to watch myself.

> The twenty-six-year-old South African, raised by a single mother, has defied the odds—race, sexuality, and disability—to gain a full scholarship to Oxford. He studies here at the Blavatnik School of Government, an incubator for future leaders. During lectures, a helper

takes notes because Eddie can't use his hands. But his disability hasn't stopped him becoming class president.

Of course, like any good journalist, Neave had interviewed a representative from the university. I was struck by how poorly the university came across, casually equating my needs with those of my nondisabled peers as if they were one and the same and reinforcing that I was not the only student struggling with financial aid. It was a full-on "All Lives Matter" moment. I couldn't help but think how dismissive this was of the unique challenges faced by disabled students at large.

But then something unexpected happened. As I watched my friends' reactions to the segment, I saw a newfound appreciation in their eyes for the trials and tribulations I had faced. I watched them have their own "ah-ha" moment, as they nodded with understanding and held one another closer for safety on my behalf.

I felt a wave of gratitude wash over me as I realized that my story, my journey, had a purpose beyond just my own education. It was a testament to the strength and perseverance of the disabled community, a rallying cry for change.

In that moment, surrounded by my closest friends, I knew that the road ahead would be a difficult one, but I was determined to continue my fight, to advocate for those who couldn't speak for themselves. For in that small dorm room, watching myself on the news, my true community was beside me, and they would stand by me every step of the way.

Eddie hopes for a time when he's no longer an exception to the norm, a world where efforts to access education don't leave him stranded. A world calibrated to suit everyone's needs. Neave Barker, Al Jazeera, Oxford.

FOURTEEN

As THE HARSH RAYS OF sunlight poured through the cafeteria window, Auntie Viv asked, "Eddie, can you see the spreadsheet okay?" With a nod and a mumbled "yeah," I gazed at the computer screen, struggling to comprehend the intricate web of mathematical calculations before me. Sensing my distraction, Auntie Viv slid her chair to the left, creating more room so I could have a clearer view. I leaned in, trying to make sense of the complex layout before me.

Auntie Viv paused, taking a bite out of her granola bar before adding, "I'll give you a moment to study it."

I meticulously examined each line item, the math appearing to align with the sequence of events thus far. The Al Jazeera feature that had aired two months prior. In response, Oxford offered to waive the costs associated with my care aides' rooms, reducing its bill from £80,000 to the original amount of £66,000. They also granted me a £5,000 "hardship" grant that was reserved for students in extenuating circumstances. I couldn't help but feel grateful for Oxford's support, but I was also aware that I still had £61,000 to fundraise.

The attention from my classmates had started to wane, and a general fatigue around the matter had settled in across campus. The buzz had died down, but the expectation for me to continue fundraising remained. After a month into the second semester, I had managed to fundraise just over £11,000, mostly from my ever-supportive ALA network, but my target still stood at £49,000. The weight of my situation felt enormous, much as Sisyphus's boulder must have felt to him, and I couldn't help but wonder if my own boulder would also roll back down the mountain.

"Thanks," I finally said, glancing toward Auntie Viv before surveying the squad across the table. They were my unwavering supporters, the last remnants of my dwindling cohort. I let out a sigh and said, "Now I have to find £50,000." My words were tinged with sarcasm, the weight of my predicament palpable in the air.

Aïda, sensing my frustration, tilted her head and offered, "One bite at a time, my dear. Remember, how does one eat an elephant?"

I mustered a smile. "Exactly, one bite at a time," I replied. Our shared laughter dissipated the tension, providing a momentary respite from the gravity of the situation. I gazed at the spreadsheet, fixating on the sum of £11,000 that I had managed to gather thus far. I mused, "I wish I could embrace each and every person who contributed. Their support means more to me than they'll ever know."

Jess, ever the jester, quipped, "Well, you'll have to hug *The Director* too."

I gaped, "No way! How much did she donate?" Tebs erupted in laughter as I squinted at the spreadsheet, searching for her name. The endowment of the school was separate from individual contributions, so I couldn't imagine *The Director* offering any of her hard-earned currency for my cause.

Auntie Viv revealed, "Fifty pounds," eliciting a chuckle from Tebs.

Tebs jested, "If I were her, I'd have marked myself as anonymous. Now everyone who scrolls through the site can see that she's a tightwad."

I replied, "I bet she'd justify it by saying every penny counts." I added, "To prove that I'm not petty, I'll give her a big hug tonight at the soiree." The school was to host a cocktail reception later that evening to honor its most influential donors and partners, and as the student body president, I was to deliver remarks on behalf of my classmates. But rumors had reached me that *The Director* was uneasy about my delivery of the student keynote, lest I use the opportunity to promote my fundraising drive to the wealthy attendees. She feared that I would cast the school in an unfavorable light. Little did she know that I possessed the fortitude to rise above such petty concerns.

As Aïda asked about my outfit for the evening, I nodded, my thoughts already drifting to the sleek black tuxedo I had picked out. The turtleneck offered a touch of sophistication, and the tuxedo, with its tailored fit, promised to hug my curves in all the right places.

"Get ready for that to be another talking point," Tebs interjected with a sly grin.

I rolled my eyes, but inside I was already bracing myself for the attention. Recently, my hair had been dyed a rich, deep hue that had caused a stir among some of the students. A classmate had taken issue with my change in appearance and made a baseless accusation that I was mismanaging my funds. The absurdity of the argument left me shaking my head in disbelief. The underlying logic was that all of my resources should go toward survival and that I shouldn't be allowed to look good or feel good while others suffered. The thought was that I should suffer until someone deemed otherwise. If I dared to present myself in a polished manner, I could no longer be considered "truly disabled." By embracing my disabled identity and being unapologetically fabulous, I had apparently forfeited my claim to vulnerability and empathy. Society believed that to truly be disabled, one must constantly perform hardship.

But I refused to play along. Looking good was a passion that ran deep within me. As a child, I dreamed of becoming a fashion designer, mesmerized by the lavish fashion empire depicted in the American soap opera *The Bold and the Beautiful*.

Sipping Dom Pérignon Through a Straw

The show's recurring shots of sketches of women in magnificent gowns, set against large wooden easels, left me in awe. I lived vicariously through the Forrester family and dreamed of one day being a part of the fashion world. I was so enthralled by the sketches that my mother eventually bought me my own easel, sketchpad, and set of pencils in every size and shape so I could try my hand at drawing. It turned out I had a natural talent for it. But as my physical strength started to decline, even the simple act of writing became a Herculean task. The decline of my body forced me to reevaluate my dreams and find new ones that were in line with my changing abilities.

"I'm going to dress to kill," I declared to Tebs with a mischievous twinkle in my eye.

As we made our way to our respective rooms, I couldn't help but feel a flutter of excitement in my chest. Standing in front of the mirror later that evening, I was met with Seven's smiling reflection as she stood behind me, straightening my bow tie. Seven was the first care aide I really connected with. Her Jamaican accent, infectious laughter, and zest for life made her stand out from the rest. She saw me for who I truly was and showed just how effortless that could be. It was Seven who had encouraged me to prioritize self-care when I was feeling low about my financial struggles. One morning, she brought posters of Prince and Beyoncé and put them up on my walls to brighten up my space. She referred to me as either Prince Edward or Queen Edwina, and the sound of her hearty laughter filled the room.

"If you could dye your hair any color, what color would you choose?" she asked, her eyes sparkling with amusement.

I paused to consider the question seriously. "I think I'd go for a caramelly...brownish...golden blond. Something that would make my complexion pop," I said, imagining the warm, golden tones that would complement my skin.

Seven disentangled herself from the bed, a fluid movement befitting her grace. "I shall return shortly," she declared, and made her way toward the door. Upon her return, she held a box of Dark and Lovely hair dye, the exact hue I had hoped for. Hours were spent bent over the sink as Seven transformed my tresses, giving birth to a hairstyle that would soon set tongues wagging among my classmates.

"You're all set," Seven said with a smile, admiring our reflection in the mirror.

I had taken great care in preparing for my address, honing my skills with the guidance of Seven, who possessed a talent for oratory. Yet as the festivities commenced, I found myself seized by nervousness, my teeth involuntarily biting at the flesh of my lips. Jess, ever observant, leaned in and whispered comfortingly, "You've got this, boo." She tilted a glass of champagne into my mouth, saying, "Here, have some liquid courage." I took a large swallow, fortifying myself for the task ahead. Aïda, standing steadfast behind me, offered a squeeze of encouragement to my shoulder.

With steady hands, I propelled my wheelchair toward the stage, climbing the steep ramp with determined effort. I took my place at the microphone stand, the height adjusted to my needs, and gazed out upon the assembly of guests. My eyes met those of *The Director*, and I drew in a deep breath, elevating my chin with newfound confidence. I summoned all the poise and sophistication within me and delivered my address, every eye in the hall upon me. When I was done, the floorboards shook with the thunderous applause of the guests. *The Director* approached, cracking a smile, and declared, "That was exquisite."

I know, I thought, which I'd never have said out loud, obviously, but I knew I did well and felt vindicated that I pulled it off despite others' expectations. Jess was on hand with a glass of champagne as soon as I landed my wheels on more secure ground. "You ate that up, boo. Freaking fantastic," she said. Then we joined the rest of the squad, who'd claimed a cocktail table for us to mingle around.

A bit later in the evening, our Nigerian classmate meandered over to us as though he'd just been informed of the most salivating piece of gossip. "Guys, you won't believe this, but you see that man standing over there?" he said, gesturing toward a rather good-looking gentleman in a tuxedo standing at the table adjacent to ours.

"The bald guy with the black frames?" I inquired.

"Yep," he confirmed. "I was standing next to him while you were giving your speech, Eddie, and he was like, 'That guy's really eloquent.' So I start telling him all about you, right? And I give him the whole fucking spiel about your fundraiser. Then he looks at me and says, 'I'd like to help him out with that!'" Our classmate brandished what looked like a type of cognac in his hand, ready to toast the moment.

"Shut the front door," I said, in total disbelief.

Auntie Viv squealed and asked the identity of this benefactor. Our Nigerian classmate took a swig. "He's a billionaire hedge fund manager. Apparently one of the school's biggest donors." The chatter among us went up several decibels.

"Shhh, guys, not so loud, he's standing right behind you, Eddie," Tebs said.

I swiveled my chair as discreetly as I could, hoping to get a better look at *The Billionaire*. Our eyes met. Then I quickly turned back. "Shit."

"Girl, too late, he's walking over to you now," Tebs said. *The Billionaire* glided in our direction as my friends sprinted out of view. I was now left to my own devices.

"You are a gifted speaker, young man," the gentleman remarked, his words causing a warm flush to rise in my cheeks. He then struck a commanding pose, his arms folded and legs braced apart, the sort of stance one sees powerful men adopt before sealing £1 million deals on television. Our conversation flowed easily and, fueled by my eagerness to impress, I presented a comprehensive overview of my professional journey thus far. He listened with keen interest, his unassuming demeanor disarming me and allowing me to reveal candidly the financial difficulties I faced at the university.

With a slight adjustment of his thick-rimmed spectacles, he asked, "How much do you require?"

"Fifty thousand pounds, sir," I replied, my voice barely above a whisper.

"It's done," he declared matter-of-factly.

I was struck speechless by his generosity. Stammering my gratitude, I said, "Th-thank you so much, sir. This means more to me than I can express."

Our conversation concluded with a firm promise that he would follow up with *The Director* the following day, and with a gracious nod, *The Billionaire* moved on to continue networking at the event.

I was momentarily dazed, blinking fast to ensure I was not in the midst of a dream. Something about the interaction felt totally absurd. I knew for a fact that nowhere in the world was something like this happening—a disabled student soliciting money from a billionaire. Yet, that easily, my financial turmoil was done. I thought of what this chance encounter may have afforded me just four months ago, my peace of mind, the time to find client-centric care, and more afternoons sipping Dom Pérignon (not the cheap stuff) at the Randolph Hotel. Overcome with joy, I spun and skidded toward my friends, breaking into celebratory circles as they cheered and clapped.

The next day, I was summoned to meet with *The Deputy* in his office. I assumed he would assist me in finalizing the administrative details for the funds to be disbursed promptly. As I floated through the halls, greeted by smiles from all those I passed, I felt a sense of peace wash over me. *The Deputy* was engrossed in a document as I entered his office, but upon my greeting, he cast the paper aside and donned a friendly grin.

"Eddie, come in," he said, motioning for me to take a seat. I eagerly complied. I was finally eager to put the monthslong matter to rest.

"I heard the good news from last night. I am deeply grateful," I said, unable to conceal my excitement.

The Deputy leaned forward, his fingers interlaced. "Yes, about that," he began, and then proceeded to deliver a devastating blow. Following a secret meeting between *The Director* and *The Billionaire*, a new agreement had been reached on my behalf. Instead of full sponsorship, I was to continue my fundraising efforts for four more months, and only then would *The Billionaire* provide the remaining funds. I'd thought I could take him at his word—after all, £50,000 would be nothing to him. But now, I sat there, regretting not having asked him to solidify his commitment that I was done having to fundraise in writing.

"We'll continue to support you and promote your campaign on our website," *The Deputy* added, his smile now irksome. While my classmates leisurely enjoyed the old books at the Bodleian, pints at King's Arms, and leisurely strolls on Port Meadow, I was in my room crafting Facebook status after Facebook status and monitoring how many times my crowdfunding link had been circulated. The thought of having to climb even higher was overwhelming, the exhaustion and trauma palpable.

With a heavy heart, I looked away from *The Deputy* and replied resignedly, "Thank you for clarifying, sir."

FIFTEEN

IN THE AFTERMATH OF THE rug being unceremoniously yanked from beneath my wheels, I was beset by a sense of hopelessness. The skies of England, usually so sullen, seemed to reflect my mood as I brooded on my lot in life. I was a disabled Black man, and Oxford, the bastion of knowledge, was where I had sought validation, only to be met with condescension and the weight of unspoken expectations. My anger simmered beneath the surface, directed at the institution that dared to think it was doing me a favor by admitting me and at myself for not being able to rise above it all.

It was on one of those gloomy days that an invitation to attend the World Economic Forum's annual regional conference in Durban, South Africa, arrived in my inbox. This gathering of global leaders, heads of state, and power brokers of the African continent was my chance to prove to the world, and to myself, that I was already outperforming ableist definitions of success long before the doors of Oxford had opened for me.

The journey to Durban was not without its obstacles. The care agency refused to provide an aide. I figured that one of my professors, a famed scholar in geopolitics who made a career for himself researching Africa's postcolonial resource allocation, might be able to help me identify sponsorship to cover my travel expenses. So I shot him an email. I received a speedy response, a telltale sign of either very good or very bad news. To my surprise, I was mistakenly copied to his executive assistant, in which he said that I was "full of crap" and didn't "stand a chance in hell" of going. I considered my request denied. But I was undaunted, driven by the fierce determination to not let anyone else dictate my life. With the help of my dear friend Thandie, who was covering the event as a member of the press corps, we secured our tickets to Durban and set off on our journey.

As I settled into my seat on the train from Oxford to Heathrow, I couldn't help but feel a sense of excitement and nervousness. My new companion, Eight, sat across from me, the phone clutched tightly in his hand. The sound of the ringing phone broke the relative silence of the carriage, and I watched as Eight answered, placing it on speaker.

The voice on the other end of the line was agitated, demanding to know where we were headed and why we had left without letting the agency know. I gazed out the window at the rolling green hills and quaint villages that surrounded us, my mind fixated on the defiant step I was about to undertake.

Eight calmly reassured the caller that we would be back by the end of the week, but the tension in his voice was palpable. I was well aware that this trip to the airport was an act of rebellion, a deliberate thumbing of my nose at the societal norms and expectations that sought to hold me back because of my disability.

As the train chugged along, I closed my eyes and took in the sights and sounds of the passing scenery. The rhythmic swaying of the carriage and the clacking of the wheels on the tracks seemed to echo the beating of my heart, each beat a testament to my determination and courage. I was sick of playing by the rules, tired of being told what I could and could not do because of my disability.

The train chugged forward, the wheels beating a mournful tune that echoed the lamentations of my heart. Seven, my former care aide, was on my mind as I journeyed toward Heathrow, bound for Durban and the company of world leaders. She had left to tend to her sickly mother in Jamaica, leaving a void in my life that could not be filled. I could still feel the tears on my cheeks as we said goodbye, as if the memory threatened to evaporate just as easily. Seven had been more than just a care aide: she was a friend, a confidante, and a fierce advocate for my independence.

Now I was on this journey with Eight, a quiet, older man who respected my agency, but the ghost of Seven was still with me. Still, I was filled with a sense of purpose as I traveled toward Heathrow, bound for Durban to rub elbows with world leaders. I was a disabled achiever, determined to shatter the walls of ableism and show the world what was possible.

But as I prepared to take flight, the reality of my financial struggles was always present, like a weight on my chest. I had raised an additional £30,000 but still had £20,000 left to raise to cover the costs of my survival—a cruel irony, as it was the same amount by which I had fought so hard to have my scholarship adjusted to reflect my needs. I was losing steam and time, and I could no longer count on *The Billionaire's* word to keep his newly adjusted promise to underwrite my costs.

As the train chugged into the station, I took a deep breath and let the memories of Seven fill me, like the sun filling the sky. The struggle was real, but I had no choice but to press on. This trip was my way of saying "screw you" to ableism, and I was ready to face whatever challenges lay ahead with strength and determination.

The plane touched down in Durban, and as I stepped out into the African sun shining over the coastal city, anticipation and excitement swelled within me. I was here to attend high-level panels on the major issues affecting the economies of Africa in the global context, and I was ready to make a difference.

The ride from the airport to the hotel was serene, lulled

by the gentle whispers of the wind. It was as if the land itself were embracing me, lifting the weight of my struggles from my shoulders. I was no longer just a student of public policy: I was a practitioner, ready to take on the world with determination and purpose.

At the hotel, I made my way to the champagne bar, where Thandie awaited. She stood, her arms outstretched for a warm embrace, and as we hugged, I couldn't help but reflect on the journey that had brought me to this moment. After months away from the African speaking circuit to focus on my studies, I was here, ready to contribute and to have a voice in shaping its future.

The sight of Thandie's face was a welcome relief as I sat across from her for the first time since beginning my graduate degree. Her glamour and go-getter attitude were traits I had missed greatly. As we hugged, her eyes were as moist as my own. "My dear, you've put on some weight," she said with a chuckle, teasing me. "I must ask your caregiver what he's been feeding you."

We settled in at the table, and Thandie revealed she had taken the liberty of ordering some champagne for us. "I need it after the day I've had," she said with a sigh. "I interviewed the Zimbabwean president earlier, and the man is so ancient he took two hours just to formulate one sentence."

Thandie then moved the conversation to my crowdfunding campaign, informing me that she had already shared it with some wealthy friends of hers. "Fingers crossed," she added.

"Rich people seem much stingier nowadays. I mean, *The Billionaire*, tuh!" She then reached for a straw, dunking it into my glass of champagne as she spoke.

"Now, my dear, tell me where you're at with the money," Thandie asked, her tone a mix of playfulness and genuine concern.

"Twenty grand," I said, taking a swig from my drink. "It's hard to believe that such a sum is now just a fraction of what I need for my education." I gazed out the window, watching as the setting sun painted the sky a warm orange hue.

Thandie chuckled, shaking her head in disbelief. "You make it sound like it's such a big deal, but to a wealthy institution like Oxford, £20,000 is just pocket change." She took a sip of her wine, making a face as a drop escaped her lips.

She leaned in, her voice lowering with a hint of anger. "I'm still so mad at them, you know. How did things get so out of hand? And I know you say confronting them won't do any good, but it still bugs me."

I nodded, understanding where she was coming from. "I get it, Thandie. Despite their vast resources, this amount is still a burden for me. The lack of trust I've encountered has been rough. But if I can just raise the rest of the funds I need, I'll be able to put this all behind me and move forward." The clink of glasses and the murmur of nearby conversations filled the air as I locked my lips with my drink, taking a slow, steady sip.

"Darling, you're writing finals in a few weeks. They promised to underwrite the rest, or whatever they're calling it. I mean, Eddie, you're whip-smart, but even you can't afford to be distracted right now."

I cleared my throat. "A promise is only a promise if the person who makes it is capable of keeping it," I said.

She shrugged and took a gulp of wine, dragging it like a cigarette, and slumped back into her chair. "All that work that you and Adrian did and you're right back where you started. Have you heard from him?" she asked.

I nodded. "We text sometimes and keep up with each other's lives on socials, but because he's moved back in with his parents in Nigeria and I'm dealing with my stuff, it's not the same as it used to be."

Thandie nodded slowly, rimming her glass with her finger curiously. "Adrian told me what happened at the club the week before you left for Oxford. I'm so sorry, darling. But as heartbreaking as this year has been for you, having Lucky with you would have made things worse. You can't let that drive a wedge into your friendship on top of everything else," she said.

Thandie was right. The potential heartache of a quasi-romantic relationship with Lucky would have been too much for me to bear on top of the heartache of institutional neglect. "I probably dodged a bullet with Lucky," I told Thandie. "But you can't deny that he was an amazing caregiver. One of the best I've ever had," I said.

Thandie looked past my shoulder, her gaze fixed on someone, and she said, "Oh my God, Eddie. You were in love with him." And just as she spoke those words, a man with a commanding presence emerged from the side, reaching out to Thandie with an extended hand, eager to greet her. The conversation shifted, but the memory of Lucky stayed with me, a reminder of the heartache and growth that came with my journey. As Thandie rose to her feet, I recognized the man as a well-known South African government official, someone I had seen countless times on television during my upbringing.

As the official turned to me, I braced myself for the customary handshake that so often left me feeling as though I was being embalmed. But before I could offer an apology for my inability to shake hands, the official's upright reflexes kicked in. In what could have only been the fight or flight of sharing space with a disabled person, his outstretched hand suddenly made contact with my face, a maneuver that looked like a slap, sounded like a slap, and felt like a slap. When it became apparent from the tortured look on my face that he had just committed an egregious faux pas, everyone froze. He, the perpetrator, froze. Thandie, the bystander, froze. I, the victim, of course froze. We all stood there, adrift, like a gargantuan iceberg off the coast of southern Africa, all frozen.

Just when I thought the entire ship was about to sink, my own non-upright tendencies kicked in, and I apologetically changed the subject. The slap was humiliating, but I'd been dealt bigger blows. I had a choice. I could leave that moment being thought of as a stoic diplomat for moving things along or a bitter prick for challenging the violation, a choice that marginalized people are often forced into in the face of micro-and macro-aggressions. So I filed the slap away and fixed my face, realigning my mask to its original place, and navigated the rest of the forum with none the wiser.

SIXTEEN

I HAD RECENTLY RETURNED FROM DURBAN, my mind brimming with inspiration from the World Economic Forum. As I made my way to the cafeteria for lunch, fate intervened. I encountered the professor who had tried to curse my trip in the hallway.

"Ah, I see you didn't make it to the forum," he said with a sly smile, as if relishing in my supposed failure.

"Actually, Professor," I replied with a grin of my own. "I did make it to Durban. Thanks for the vote of confidence."

The color drained from his face as he realized his mistake. "Well, congratulations," he stammered.

"Thank you," I said with a nod, before continuing on my way to the cafeteria. Little did I know that my travels to

Durban had made me the talk of the school and that a new chapter of my journey was about to unfold.

I had just missed the lunch rush. As I entered the cafeteria, I was met with a palpable air of discontent from the stragglers exiting. The students I had only recently called peers now glared at me with annoyance. The word across campus was that it was audacious of me to still expect their pity—or so I'd been told. Yet there were a few who remained steadfast: my squad, who stood by me even amid the judgment of the others. Despite not feeling hungry, I made my way to the window and gazed out at the bustling campus life. The searing cold outside did nothing to ease the chill I felt deep within my soul. Tears streamed down my face as I reflected on my existence at Oxford, feeling like an unwanted transplant organ, rejected and out of place. I had returned from hobnobbing with world leaders, feeling like a conqueror, basking in the glow of my hard-won achievements. But as I stepped back into the daily grind of surviving ableism, the veneer of success began to peel away. Every little indignity that I'd learned to brush off with a smile came crashing down on me, reminding me of the chasm between my outward success and the struggle of simply existing in a world not built for me.

The elevator that was too small to accommodate my wheelchair, the lack of accessible restrooms, the sidelong glances of strangers who saw my disability before they saw me. All of these small cuts added up, leaving me feeling drained and defeated. I wondered if I would ever truly escape the shadow of nonupright sensibilities, if I would ever be able to simply live in a world that accepted me as I am. I buried my chin in my scarf, contemplating if it was time to break away from this fundraising drive that was consuming my life. The thought of finally finding peace with the world and myself weighed heavily on my mind.

"Eddie?" a voice whispered softly, as I sat with my eyes closed, tears streaming down my face. I slowly opened my lids, my vision blurring before slowly coming into focus. I tilted my head back, resting it against the headrest of my wheelchair, gathering my thoughts. "Eddie. Why the tears, man? What's up?"

It was Noam, my newfound friend and a Rhodes scholar. Our paths had crossed at a cocktail function in London months prior, and we quickly hit it off. With his quirky sense of style—at the time he was sporting a dark suit paired with a candy-floss-pink shirt and floral bow tie—Noam was the epitome of confident individuality. Of all the people I met in my early days at Oxford, Noam was the most open-minded, a trait I highly valued. Although we both studied in the same building, our lives couldn't have been more different—he was ensconced upstairs in the doctoral program, while my own chaos unfolded downstairs in the master's program.

But here he was, walking in on me in the midst of my breakdown, and I felt an overwhelming urge to confide in him. I shared with him my struggles—from the neglect of my caregivers and *The Billionaire* who reneged on his promise to fund my care, to my current state, in which I was still £20,000 short of my fundraising goal.

"Whoa, Eddie, I had no idea it was this bad. I'm so sorry, man. I wish you'd told me sooner," Noam said, his eyes scanning the room as if searching for answers. Then, with a determined look, he declared, "Let's go upstairs right now and get some answers from management. We can sort this mess out together."

I appreciated Noam's unwavering support, but I was wary of roping in yet another friend to come to my aid. "Thanks, Noam, I appreciate it. But what more could you say that I haven't already tried?" I replied, my voice heavy with exhaustion.

Just then, Viv sauntered over to us, a carefree smile on her face. "I was looking for you at the library, Eddie, but you were a no-show. Hey, Noam. What's got y'all whispering like this?"

"Noam thinks we should go upstairs and confront management about this whole funding situation," I said, still feeling uncertain about the outcome.

Viv consulted the ceiling for a few seconds. "Well, honey, it couldn't hurt to try. I've known Noam a while, and he's got a way of talking that can sway even the most stubborn of folks. And we're not gonna let you suffer any longer, Eddie. We're gonna get to the bottom of this once and for all."

We set out on our mission. We made our way to the elevator and up to the second floor where management's offices were. As soon as the elevator doors parted, the receptionist's gaze was upon us. She approached with a brisk step, her eyes flickering with suspicion. Noam calmly explained that we needed to see either *The Director* or *The Deputy*, as a matter of utmost urgency.

"I see," she said with a measured tone. "Please have a seat. I will inform them of your arrival."

We took our seats in the waiting area, surrounded by curious eyes. The staff, who had peered out of their offices, now studied us with a mixture of suspicion and intrigue. Noam whispered to me, "Why are they all giving you the death stare?"

It was a question that echoed in my mind, as I gazed at the stark, sterile surroundings. The receptionist soon returned to us, like a ray of light in the gathering darkness, and informed us that *The Director* was out of town but that *The Deputy* was available to see us.

Noam led the way, his confident stride carrying us forward into the unknown. *The Deputy's* office was a study in elegance and refinement, with high ceilings and gleaming wood paneling. He looked up, surprised, as we entered. "I didn't realize you and Eddie were friends," he said to Noam.

Noam replied, "Yes, we are. And I'm deeply concerned about him. It's my understanding that the deadline for the underwriter to come through for Eddie has already passed. We're here to get some clarity on where things stand."

With a powerful voice, Auntie Viv joined in: "Yes, and Eddie has fulfilled his end of the bargain. He's continued to fundraise and brought the amount down from £61,000 to £20,000 through blood, sweat, and tears."

I watched, struck dumb by the strength of my friends, as Noam opened up a new line of inquiry. "What's the back of the envelope?" he asked, his arms folded with determination.

Viv and I instantly locked eyes. We knew, as if by telepathy, that Noam's question could only be understood as white male upright privilege. While appeals of logic and justice had fallen short, Noam had opened the conversation to a whole other playing field—money. And money was just what I needed. I knew that this was a moment that called for my absolute silence while my upright sibling stuck his neck out in solidarity.

Noam and *The Deputy* continued to speak in their coded language as if interlocked in a strange dance that only they knew the choreography to. Finally, *The Deputy* acquiesced, "Today's Friday. I have no doubt that by Monday, Eddie's bill will be settled."

And so it was. On Monday, I received an email, like a bolt from the blue, informing me that my debts had been cleared and that I was paid up in advance for the remainder of my stay in Oxford.

SEVENTEEN

I SAT IN MY ROOM, SURROUNDED by books and papers, feeling both victorious and defeated. The fight for my freedom had lasted a year, every day a battle to prove my worth and my right to be at Oxford. But now it was over, and I had emerged on the other side, bruised but not broken.

Yet as I sat at my desk, I couldn't help but wonder at what cost this victory had come. The toll it had taken on my mental and physical health was immeasurable. I was exhausted, drained of all energy and motivation. The days had blended together in a never-ending cycle of fighting, proving, and surviving.

I looked out the window, watching the clouds drift by, and thought of all the times I had doubted myself. The moments of self-doubt that had threatened to consume me, the moments when I thought I couldn't go on. But I had pushed through, I had refused to give up, and now here I was, a grad student at Oxford, with a future full of endless possibilities.

And so I took a deep breath, feeling the weight of the year lift off my shoulders, and I whispered a silent thank-you to the whatever higher power might be listening for allowing me to barely scrape by and for the love and support of my friends, my only saving grace.

Yes, the fight had been long and hard, but I had won. And though I was exhausted, I knew that the energy and motivation would return, for I was a fighter, a survivor, and I was ready to face whatever lay ahead.

My eyes lingered on the bronze statue of a military officer on horseback, a symbol of a bygone era, and then to the flickering cursor on my Facebook page, a reminder of the loneliness that pervaded my life. I considered the words to accompany a picture of my Oxford alumni card, a badge of blue and white with my own face, symbolizing my association with a community I'd struggled to fit into.

I never thought that the hardships I faced would become the basis for my thesis. My aim was to critically examine the limitations of reasonable accommodation as a public policy tool for the rights of people with disabilities. Through my experiences navigating institutional life with a disability, I learned that just as a whale cannot be comfortably accommodated in a swimming pool, disabled individuals cannot be reasonably accommodated without systemic interventions to address ableism. Compliance alone is not enough to ensure our dignity and agency.

"Wake up," I said, activating my laptop's voice recognition system. The watermarked, algorithmic prompt in the text box instructed me to speak what was on my mind. But with the words on the tip of my tongue, I proceeded to dictate instead what was in my heart:

Quite possibly the hardest, most painful year of my adult life. Graduating carrying more trauma in my belly than I carried when I commenced this chapter over a year ago. But I did it. I got into Oxford and got through it with my master's degree. But I'm beginning to realize that I am more expansive than any space or institution. With all that space and possibility, this journal sometimes feels hollow and empty. When I embarked on this journey, I thought I needed Oxford to feel validated and whole. What I needed then and what I need now, what I will always need, is the grace and power of my imagination. Me. Eddie Ndopu. I am not Eddie, Oxford alumnus. I am Eddie Ndopu. I've come a long way. But I'm done defining myself according to how far I've traveled or how far I have yet to travel. It's time to stay put and look within myself to embark on the greatest adventure of my life: healing.

Satisfied with my note, I gave the computer the green light to post on Facebook.

As I GAZED OUT THE window, the winding roads and stately buildings fading into a blur, my thoughts drifted toward the future. With only a few short weeks remaining before my scheduled return to South Africa, I was faced with the daunting task of putting the pieces in place for my post-graduate life. After a year of emotional exhaustion, navigating the labyrinth of caregiving and medical appointments, I longed for stability and comfort.

I was determined to find a care aide who would understand my needs and work in tandem with my mother to help me recover my strength and vitality. As I scrolled through my contacts list, my eyes landed on the name of someone who had been a source of solace in the past—Laeticia. Her profile picture, a grainy image captured years ago, was still a beacon of warmth, with her smile reaching her sparkling eyes and her pixie cut accentuating her high cheekbones. I sent a message, inquiring if she would be interested in serving as my care aide upon my return. As I hit send, I took a deep breath, fingers crossed that this arrangement would work out.

Just then, there was a knock at the door. I swiveled my wheelchair toward the entrance, calling out, "It's open." And there, standing before me, were three of the most brilliant and innovative trans artists of our time—Alok Vaid-Menon,

Sipping Dom Pérignon Through a Straw

Travis Alabanza, and Kat Kai Kol-Kes. Each of them looked like a goddess from a fantasy novel, but their cultural impact and refusal to be pigeonholed into gendered boxes were undeniably real. The Parisian couture houses could not hold a candle to their fierce fashions and dazzling style. They were like the Three Wise Men but genderqueer. And they had a gift for me.

Alok, a dear friend and fellow traveler on this journey, had called me a few weeks earlier to offer a listening ear as I struggled with my financial and emotional difficulties. The three were in the middle of a European speaking tour and were making a pit stop in Oxford to see me. The plan was to put on a photoshoot in full glam to celebrate my graduation and honor my cobblestoned path to this moment. The thought of reclaiming my experience with this shoot sent shivers down my spine, as it was a fitting way to conclude my Oxford chapter with the same sense of magic and wonder that had marked its beginning. And as I gazed into their eyes, full of love and support, I was reminded that the beauty I sought was always within me.

Alok, Travis, and Kat, each carrying luggage of different sizes and shapes, entered my room, their expressions serious and determined. Kat was the first to speak: "Darling, consider this your graduation ceremony." And with that, she pulled out a makeup kit from her suitcase. They had arrived as guardians of love and restoration, bringing with them talismans of beauty: makeup, pearls, lace, feathers, and dresses.

As I gazed upon my friends, an overwhelming sense of belonging washed over me. I had risen from the lifeless gravel after nearly succumbing to the ableism that so many people with disabilities face. And here I was, getting dolled up in all my brilliance alongside friends who, like the squad, truly understood the battle to be oneself. Warsan Shire's words echoed in my mind: "If we're gonna heal, let it be glorious." And so we titled our performance "Welcome to Your Funeral."

WE EMBARKED ON OUR PILGRIMAGE through the ancient streets of Oxford, draped in fabulous attire. Though we were met with the leering stares of onlookers, I drew fortitude from the fact that I was not alone. As we approached the Radcliffe Camera, I rolled my wheelchair forward, defiant and determined to show the world that disabled bodies are deserving of intellectual curiosity and the education to foster it. Posing in front of the camera was an exercise in agency. I wasn't appealing for the benevolence of strangers to fund my care or making a case for a global news outlet. Instead, this was my moment to be playful, to be irreverent, to be myself.

Just a short distance away, the Sheldonian Theatre was a sight to behold, its grand facade a testament to the rich history of the university. And yet disabled voices had been ignored and sidelined for far too long. But with my friends by my side, I stood tall, my head held high, and claimed my rightful place in history with some solo shots.

Sipping Dom Pérignon Through a Straw

The Bodleian Library was next, its shelves upon shelves of books inviting us to explore the infinite possibilities that lay ahead. My disability was a source of strength, and I refused to be limited by society's narrow understanding.

At Christ Church College, we celebrated in the love and support of our friends. We huddled together, posing and throwing our heads back like Hollywood starlets captured on candid camera. The majestic spires of the college rose toward the sky, reminding us of the limitless potential that lay ahead. Here, staring down the camera with my larger-than-life contemporaries, I was filled with peace, knowing that no matter what the future held, I would always be accepted and loved for exactly who I am.

Finally, I arrived at the Blavatnik School of Government, the site of my yearlong trial. The imposing building loomed before me, a monolith of glass and steel. In that moment, I realized that my journey had come a full circle. I had faced my fears, overcome my struggles, and emerged victorious. The photographer captured the moment as I sat there, lost in contemplation, the sun sinking low on the horizon, casting long shadows across the grounds.

EIGHTEEN

A WOMAN APPROACHED ME WITH A walkie-talkie headset. She knelt beside me, her gangly frame balancing against the side of my wheelchair. "Mr. Ndopu, I am Carolina," she said, her voice soft and warm. "I'm a member of the production crew. Once President Obama and Mr. Benioff finish their talk, I'll escort you to the VIP reception." I nodded, exchanging a look of excitement with Mom, who sat beside me. Laeticia, who had been dozing off, was now wide awake, her eyes sparkling with anticipation as she gazed at the stage behind Carolina.

The air was charged with energy as the announcer declared, "Ladies and gentlemen, please put your hands together for Salesforce Founder, Chairman, and CEO Marc Benioff." He stepped onto the stage, a full-figured man dressed in a navy suit, his hair slicked back and curling at the ends. He boomed into the microphone, "Y'all ready?" The crowd erupted as President Obama joined him onstage, the two friends embracing in a bro handshake.

The conversation that followed was warm, witty, and wise. The mutual admiration between the two was palpable, with President Obama making the audience laugh with his humorous take on the challenges of leadership. "When I was president, I learned that by the time a problem reached my desk, it meant that someone else down the chain of command could not solve it. Poop rolls uphill," he quipped, his eyes scanning the sea of faces beaming back at him.

As the conversation came to an end, I searched for Carolina in the crowd. Just as the audience rose to their feet for a standing ovation, she appeared beside me, tapping my shoulder. "Mr. Ndopu, please follow me." Mom, Laeticia, and I followed her through a door that opened up to an indoor gazebo, draped in white. Inside, President Obama awaited us, his megawatt smile illuminating the room. Despite the lack of fanfare, the aura of his presence was palpable, a reminder of the historic figure he was, the first Black president of the United States.

As I locked eyes with President Obama, trepidation began to creep up within me. I couldn't bear to have a repeat performance of what had happened in Durban two years before, causing me to whisper under my breath as he made his way toward me, "Please don't attempt to shake my hand, Mr. President."

Sipping Dom Pérignon Through a Straw

I'd spent the last two years since graduating focused on processing my Oxford experience and getting back to feeling like my fabulous self. And I made sure it was glorious. I sat in the cockpit of a Piper as the pilot somersaulted above Mozambique's Port of Maputo. I slept fifteen hours straight, on several occasions. I traveled to Rwanda, the land of a thousand hills, where I guest taught a local math class, ironically my least favorite subject growing up, for the sweetest group of disabled children in a village north of Kigali as part of my humanitarian work for the Nobel Peace Prize–winning organization Humanity and Inclusion. I got blissfully sloshed on a lagoon after midnight in Mauritius, where I'd looked up at the sky and was absolutely convinced that the clouds had taken the shape of a centaur. I returned to the African Leadership Academy, where I was captured on camera ugly crying at the unveiling ceremony of an elevator the institution had named after me in recognition of my human rights advocacy over the years.

With new opportunities flowing in, I'd one day answered a call from an unknown number. Good thing I did. It was the United Nations, asking me if I'd accept an appointment from the secretary-general to serve as one of his global champions for sustainable development, alongside cultural icons, heads of state, and royalty. Um, yes!

Though I didn't peg President Obama at the type to take a swing, I couldn't risk the embarrassment and weirdness of another slap, so before President Obama made any sudden movements and before I broke into a cold sweat from anxiety, I filled the space between us with pleasantries to deflect his attention from my deformed, but otherwise glorious, hands. Halfway through my monologue, he spotted a photographer who had been lurking behind us. "Let's take a picture," he said, bending down to put his arm around my shoulder. *Whew,* I thought. Midflash, I sensed Mom's presence behind me. She was used to giving me my space to make my own impression on others, but this time, I swerved slightly and invited her into Obama's orbit. "This is my mother, Mr. President," I said.

The disability justice gods must have been smiling down on me, as the handshake I feared President Obama intended to give me was now redirected to Mom. "Nice to meet you, Mr. President," Mom said, accepting the greeting. Ever graceful, she broke the ice, reminding President Obama of his recent trip to South Africa, where he'd publicly confessed to underestimating the highveld winter and vowed before the world's press to pack a pair of long johns the next time he returned. He was in stitches.

This was clearly Mom's moment as much as it was mine, a moment for her to be the person she'd always imagined she'd been were it not for apartheid. To this day she laments that the most painful atrocity of apartheid was less the sociopolitical oppression of Black South Africans (though that remains an unspeakable crime against humanity) and more the suppression of our ambition. When the architects of apartheid relegated Black South Africans to second-class citizenship, they not only colonized the land anew, mapping their atrocities and boundary lines after those of the Dutch and the British, but they also prevented millions of Black people bursting with brilliance and beauty from dreaming with reckless, relentless possibility. This ambition—often the bridge between a person's potential and their self-actualization—remains unfinished and abandoned, like a relic of a bygone era. It's a ruin, paved with crushed, incomplete, unpursued dreams. That I had a front-row seat to Mom's endearing interaction with arguably one of twenty-first century's most influential figures filled me with pride. It was as if she had just constructed her own goddamn bridge and crossed it. As Obama excused himself from Mom's grip to continue working the room, Salesforce CEO Marc Benioff seized the conversational opening and stepped forward to also say hello.

"Hey, man, thanks for coming. Klaus hit me up a couple weeks back, told me all about you," Marc said, casually referencing the iconic founder of the World Economic Forum with a friendly grin. "Had to have you here, man. Also mentioned you'll be joining us in Davos in a few weeks."

I was indeed planning to attend the gathering in Davos. The mere thought of it had stirred within me a sense of foreboding. Upon perusing the list of attendees, I was anxious to learn that two individuals from my recent past would also be in attendance: *The Director* and *The Billionaire*. The prospect of once more facing them—individuals whom I had not expected to encounter again—filled me with a blend of dread and uncertainty. What would seeing them mean for my healing process since graduating from Oxford? I had worked so hard to put the past behind me, to leave the wounds and scars of my experiences there firmly in the rearview mirror. I was well on my way with a dedicated, client-first care aide and a calendar stacked with equal parts diplomacy and rest. And yet, now here I was, about to be thrust back into the past once more.

Would I be able to maintain my composure, to carry myself with the dignity and grace that befit a graduate of Oxford? Or would the wounds of the past reopen, leaving me vulnerable and exposed once more? These were the questions that plagued me as I prepared for the gathering in Davos a few weeks later.

And yet, amid my turmoil, I took solace in the fact that I had come so far since graduating from Oxford. I was no longer the same person I was then—I was stronger, more resilient, and better equipped to face whatever lay ahead.

NINETEEN

AS THE ROAD WOUND STEEPLY upward, the jalopy I rode in leaned precariously back. Our chauffeur, Marcus, caught my wince in the rearview mirror. "Is all well back there?" he inquired, rousing Mom and Laeticia from their slumber.

"I'm fine," I answered, masking my discomfort. But the truth was far from fine. I struggled to keep my balance, clinging to what little strength remained as I braced against the jostling of the rickety vehicle. The Swiss Alps were not kind, their rough roads testing my mettle at every turn. No matter how much I wished for smoother terrain, the unforgiving mountains remained steadfast. Just as I feared I could endure no more, the van leveled out onto flatter ground and I breathed a sigh of relief.

As we crept through the snow-dusted streets of Davos, I

couldn't ignore the historic significance of this mountain town. It was here in 1993 that Nelson Mandela and F. W. de Klerk joined hands in a momentous show of unity that foretold the end of apartheid. It was in Davos, at the dawn of a new century, that Bill Gates helped conceive the Global Alliance for Vaccines and Immunization, an organization that has since saved nearly a billion lives through lifesaving vaccines. And it was here, amid the turmoil of the 2008 financial crisis, that financiers came to lick their wounds, surrounded by the snow-capped peaks and valleys.

Now, at the height of the summit's fiftieth anniversary, I stood ready to face *The Director* and *The Billionaire*, and to find closure on my journey of healing since Oxford.

Marcus zigzagged the van through the impossible streets, narrowly dodging the taillights of the Maybachs clogging traffic. As I gazed out the window to take inventory of my picturesque surroundings, the sunken black sedans slithered along the roads. I envied the uprights who sat veiled in those seductive cars by the tinted windows. I reluctantly peeked at the clock on the dash. My speaking engagement, covering everything from climate change to the kitchen sink, was in thirty minutes. The plan was to get to the venue ahead of all the uprights so I could take my time doing disabled things without being gawked at. But that plan had dissolved as we'd all needfully overslept the night before. When the clock and traffic decide to fight it out in Davos, you are almost certain to get caught in the crossfire, no matter who you are. Whether a member of the British royal family, a Silicon Valley CEO, or a G7 head of state, the mountain doesn't care. The most sensible thing to do now was take a deep breath, practice some grace, and hope we didn't skid into a patch of black ice.

Mom and Laeticia, who were now awake and perched on the edge of the seats in the last row of the van, braced themselves for the logistical ritual they knew all too well. No one spoke. We were surviving entirely on the adrenaline of getting through a jam-packed itinerary. Each of us was painfully aware of the fact that one of the biggest milestones of my career was minutes away from slipping through my fingers—or, more aptly, my one good finger.

The exterior of the Panorama Hotel, where my talk was scheduled, was somewhat deceptive. From the van, the building's underwhelming sliding doors looked more like an upmarket corner store than a hotel that was playing host to the world's most powerful people. I watched a trail of attendees slip inside, but unlike my VVIP counterparts, who easily dashed out of their limousines as they rounded the bend, I had to wait for Marcus to park in the hotel driveway, circle his way around the body of the car, and climb into the trunk so that he could then dismount my wheelchair from the van's floorboard. It was a laborious operation that added at least five minutes to the clock. Five minutes I didn't have.

As Marcus dashed out of the vehicle, my phone rang. Laeticia whipped it out of my navy blue Davos-embossed briefcase, clambered over the seats, and pressed it against my right ear. "I just arrived," I said with a tinge of anguish in my voice. "See you in a bit," I added. Ryan, the organizer of the high-level event I was running late for, continued talking on the other line, but I barely could make out what he'd been saying. Laeticia had stretched her arm out as far as it could go, but Ryan's slightly panicked voice all but disappeared as I began backing up down the ramp.

"Okay, sweetheart, go straight," Mom said from behind me, as she directed me to land my wheels carefully on the slushy-snow-covered ground with all the precision of an air traffic controller. A competent pilot after more than two decades at the wheel, I sashayed gracefully down. I might have been late, but I was still mindful of my angles. We wouldn't have wanted a compromising shot of yours truly appearing in the *Financial Times*.

"Call me when you are done," Marcus said, as he slammed the trunk door. "I'll pick you up in the same spot." I swiveled sharply and charged toward the lobby of the unassuming hotel, Mom and Laeticia trailing behind me, all of us doing our best to dodge the icy spots. If I could, I'd have simply teleported and found myself onstage, but instead, my wheeled ways required a different kind of journey.

"Are you going to the Dome?" asked a casually dressed man sporting a tuft of blonde hair so dry that it looked like hay. I nodded. He led us behind the concierge desk, through a maze of tiny corridors. Before I knew it we were navigating an industrial kitchen. We squeezed ourselves between cooks and servers who were yelling to each other over the sounds of pots and pans crashing against appliances and utensils. The rich aroma of freshly blended herbs and marinated meats bounced just as loudly off the walls.

We emerged from the kitchen into the florescent light of midday. The sun reflected off the snow, functioning like natural floodlights. Then the man with the dehydrated hair pointed to a makeshift platform that was suspended above the snow-covered treetops, spanning the space between the main building of the hotel and the Dome. "Once you cross this bridge, you will see the entrance to the Dome," he said. And with that, he disappeared as mysteriously as when he'd first appeared.

At four and a half feet when seated in my chair, I cut a timid figure on top of a slope that was thousands of feet above sea level. My eyes drifted from the ski runs swiftly carrying straggling attendees to the Dome toward the wooden scaffolding I needed to traverse to get there myself. It was clear that the organizers had hastily erected this precarious plywood structure to enable me to get across. *I swear to God, this must be the most inaccessible place on the face of the Earth*, I thought, utterly astonished that this slanted platform, nine feet wide at best with no railing, was the only "bridge" available for me to access the stage on the other side of this building. Everything was slanted, including the mountain on which this godforsaken hotel had been perched.

"Is your hand okay?" Mom called out from behind me, as she breathlessly tried to keep up. I thought about it as I readied myself to cross. My hand did feel clammy over the ball nestled in my palm. But stopping now to adjust my hand was only going to slow me down further.

"Yeah, I'm good," I shouted, convincing myself that my hand was good enough to get me across. Any adjustments could be made once inside, I figured. "Let's go faster, guys. I'm so late."

Determined, I gently applied pressure to the joystick and slowly mowed over the many tiny splinters sprouting from the makeshift structure beneath me. "I've got this," I murmured. I leaned forward and applied a little more pressure on my joystick. But because the plank was slick, I completely lost my traction and center of gravity, and began to accelerate left toward the abyss.

"Eddie!" Laeticia shrieked. She screamed my name into the ether with the kind of ferocity meant to endow me with the motor-neuron function required to save myself. It didn't work. Mom ran ahead of me. And with remarkable dexterity, she yanked my hand from the joystick, which then brought my chair to a halt, way too close to the edge of the railingless bridge for comfort.

My body convulsed with terror. As I tried to regulate my distressed heartbeat, it suddenly struck me that the anxiety I'd been internalizing, the fear that because there was no way for me to straggle in unobtrusively without being gawked at, as if I were some circus act, had almost caused me to drive myself over a mountain in the Swiss Alps. And while that would have been a pretty glamorous departure, the discomforting gaze of uprights who'd never seen a drop-dead-gorgeous disabled man occupying a space like this before was not worth prematurely dying over. *When I do leave this Earth, let it be because of my body giving out to my degenerative condition,* I thought, *not because of some barely compliant Swiss scaffolding.* Mom held my jaw in the palms of her vein-ridden hands. I scrutinized her face and then said calmly, "I'm okay, Mom." With desperation inscribed on hers, she saw the determination in my face and let me go.

Laeticia peeped over Mom's shoulder. "Are you sure, Mr. Ndopu?" she asked, still shaken.

I cracked a smile. "I'm good, guys. Sorry for scaring you."

I exhaled sharply, releasing myself of the desire to control time. I continued to roll along, but this time I intentionally drove slower. As for the fact that I was now officially late-late, *to hell with it,* I told myself. Grateful to be alive, I figured anyway that my presence was worth the wait.

"These people need to do a better job. This is unacceptable," Mom protested, as we continued our trek, with caution and, eventually, success. Ryan's stout silhouette came into view as we got closer to the building. He stood at the entrance to the Dome with his hands on his hips. His half-smile, half-grimace broadcast what I imagined was his internal tug-of-war between needing to be hospitable and needing to get this show on the road.

"The man of the hour has finally arrived," he said, barely waiting for me to hoist my wheels over the four-inch lip that led up to the front door. "I hope the accessible route we designed for you worked out okay?" Ryan asked, as we navigated the labyrinthine hallways inside. I sensed Mom itching to interject.

"Let's chat about that later," I chimed in, beating her to it so as to avert a confrontation. We shuffled into the palatial room, with its soaring floor-to-ceiling views of treetops dunked in snow. My fellow panelists had already taken their seats. As if everyone in the room had all been given the same script, they all just sat and watched me. No, scratch that. They gawked at me. But seasoned at making an entrance by force, favor, or failure to accommodate, I didn't give a damn. As I climbed up the ramp onto the stage, I returned their gaze with the self-confidence of a disabled man who was fed up with accommodating basic upright sensibilities.

I surveyed the audience as I readied myself to speak. Then I spotted him, *The Billionaire*, with those unmistakable thick black frames of his, as he gazed back at me from the middle rows. I had no time to process the shock of seeing him, as the moderator opened with a question for me. So I put on my best poker face and maintained unflinching eye contact with the moderator and my fellow panelists, using the chance to wax lyrical nonstop about all sorts of stuff to avoid accidentally finding myself looking back at *The Billionaire*. For the entire program, it was as if I were suspended under a lake. The colors around me were washed out, the edges in the room blurry. It was only at the end of the panel that applause jolted me out of the water and into awareness.

Caught up in the swell, I looked out onto the audience and our eyes locked again. I immediately got cold feet. *Fuck closure,*

I thought. I visually mapped a path through the crowd that I figured would enable me to slip out undetected and, as soon as the applause sufficiently quieted, wheeled myself offstage. When I got down, I cajoled Mom and Laeticia into getting a move on so we could make a dash for the doors, but *The Billionaire* made a beeline for me faster than I was able to wheel away.

"Hey," he said, ever casual. I could tell from the way the corners of his smile twitched that he struggled to hide his surprise. I knew this was the last place on God's green Earth he'd have expected to bump into me.

"Hey," I replied, forcing myself to steady my nerves.

"Look at you," he said. Then he chuckled and shook his head. "You're looking well."

"Thanks so much. So are you," I said. My brain was foggy from the whole ordeal, and it was as if my words had abandoned me. All of the clapbacks and clever quips that I'd imagined one day being able to say to him were nowhere to be found. I just continued to grin and nod.

"Um, anyway, great job up there. Still as eloquent as ever," he said, confirming that he remembered that night he offered to cover my care costs. I heard that as an acknowledgment of his role in my struggle. It was, after all, my eloquence that had spurred him to open up his wallet that night at the public policy soiree marking the end of Michaelmas term. In the wake of learning that I still had to fundraise, I had thought that if I ever saw him again, I would need an explanation. I needed to hear that it was out of his hands, that Oxford made him withhold the funds he'd promised me, or that he had had a change of heart and didn't know if he could tell me. But as I looked at him in a hall I'd addressed on the basis of my own merit, I didn't need him to say anything further. *Still as eloquent as ever* was enough. It meant that I was thriving in spite of everything that had happened.

I held his gaze and gave him as wholehearted a smile as I'd given in a while. "I need to go, but it was really great to see you again," I said. Before stepping out of the way, he reached for his blazer's inner pocket and pulled out a business card. He turned to Mom, who was standing with Laeticia at a healthy eavesdropping distance.

"Do you have a pen?" he asked her. She nodded and retrieved one for him from her handbag. "I am going to give you my private cell phone number," he said, as he scribbled on the back of the embossed card. "Stay in touch." He tucked it behind my paisley pocket square and disappeared into the crowd.

THE FLIGHT ATTENDANT APPROACHED ME with a warm smile, revealing a gleaming set of teeth. "What can I get you to drink, Mr. Ndopu?" he inquired.

I took a deep breath and replied with a sense of quiet pride, "Dom Pérignon, please. With a straw."

He nodded, his eyes brimming with understanding, before reaching above me to press the button next to the built-in minibar. With a soft click, the gold-rimmed wooden table emerged, and the flight attendant gracefully pulled it over my lap. "I'll be right back with your champagne, sir," he promised.

We had just taken off from Davos, soaring high above the Swiss Alps, on our journey back to South Africa. That morning, as we checked out of the hotel, I caught a glimpse of *The Director* from a distance. I gazed at her but decided not to speak to her. I had survived the challenges of Oxford—I was determined to move on. And now I was standing among the world's leaders at Davos.

The flight attendant returned, his steps light as he carried a champagne flute in one hand and a chilled bottle of Dom Pérignon in the other. He placed the glass in front of me, his movements fluid and graceful, and proceeded to pour the sparkling champagne. Reaching into his shirt pocket, he retrieved a golden paper straw and placed it in the glass. "Cheers," he said, his eyes meeting mine in a moment of shared celebration. And then, with a gentle nod, he left me to savor the golden nectar in solitude.

As I took to the skies, I was reminded of all the moments when I felt like a mere shadow in the world of privilege. But as I sipped on my Dom Pérignon through a golden straw, I realized that perhaps this small act of rebellion was my way of reclaiming my humanity. A declaration that I would no longer be invisible, no longer accommodate myself to the expectations of a world that tries to confine me.

In the fleeting moments that transpired, a tall and slender man appeared on the edge of my vision. His sudden arrival disrupted the tranquil solitude of my drink, but I assumed he was merely on his way to the lavatory. However, I was wrong. With a look of curiosity, he approached me, squatting down in the aisle beside me.

"Can I help you, sir?" I said, cautiously moving away from my glass.

"Ah, sipping Dom Pérignon through a straw. Now that's cool." He quipped with a hint of humor, as if he were an intimate acquaintance of the Pérignon dynasty. Initially, his comment struck me as patronizing, as if he was commenting on a child's adorable quirk. But as he rose to his feet and sauntered back to his seat, I decided there was another way to internalize this interaction. By savoring champagne in my unconventional way, I had shattered the preconceived notions about my place in the world as a disabled person. I belonged at Davos, I belonged at Oxford, and I belonged in this first-class cabin. My dreams were valid, even if it meant fighting ableism along the way. My success was not due to conformity but because of my fierce insistence on affirming my worth.

Perhaps my boldness had encouraged my visitor to break free from his own constraints and envision a world beyond the ordinary. Perhaps, in sipping Dom Pérignon through a straw, I had just shown him a glimmer of possibility—that another more extraordinary and jaw-dropping way of existing was within grasp. And perhaps that glimmer of possibility held, for me, the essence of life, the thrill of the unknown, and a taste of what it truly means to live.

ACKNOWLEDGMENTS

MY HEART OVERFLOWS WITH AN abundance of gratitude for the incredible support and encouragement that breathed life into this memoir. Above all, I am moved to express my profound appreciation to the universe for its cosmic guidance and grounding, which have ushered me through the twists and turns of my existence. Without this force, I would not be sitting where I am today.

To my fellow disabled warriors, whose tireless pursuit of agency and self-actualization stokes the fires of my inspiration, I am indebted beyond measure. Our individual and collective struggles propel me forward, urging me to be better, to fight harder, and to tell our stories with unflinching authenticity.

Georgia Frances King, I cannot thank you enough for being

the spark that set this book ablaze. During the COVID-19 pandemic, when I was feeling lost and alone, you called me and helped me channel my emotions into constructing the book proposal that led to these pages. Your early affirmation of my writing abilities gave me the courage to share my story with the world. Bridget Matzie, I feel blessed to have a rockstar literary agent like you in my corner. We did it! Thank you for being my most ardent champion in developing my voice as a writer.

Krishan Trotman, my publishing hero, I am forever grateful for your unwavering support throughout this process. You are the kind of publisher every author dreams of working with, and I appreciate your recognition that holding me to a higher standard of outcome was not the same as holding me to an ableist standard of production. Your belief in me, your trust in my vision, provided me with the space to take my time and write this book on my own terms. Thank you for seeing me, for hearing me, and for being a true partner in this journey.

Amina Iro, my editor extraordinaire, words cannot express the depth of my gratitude for your tireless efforts in shaping this book. You are a master of your craft, and the herculean achievement, that is, this work of art is as much yours as it is mine. Your role in bringing these pages to life was so much more than simply structuring my scenes and refining my prose. You bore witness to the non-normative process that made this book possible, and you did so with tenderness, with empathy, with a fierce commitment to my voice and my story. You pushed me, you challenged me, and you validated my abilities, even when I doubted myself and broke down in tears.

Alok Vaid-Menon, my confidante, thank you for urging me to dig deeper, for challenging me to tap into emotional depths I didn't know I had, and for being a sister and comrade whose support and encouragement means the world to me. I am forever indebted to your luminous brilliance, and I will ride on your coattails for as long as I can.

To my current care team, the support structure I've been manifesting for as long as I can remember: Angie, you have my deepest appreciation for staying up with me during those restless nights when I found myself in a state of panic, racing to meet my deadlines. Jade, my kindred spirit, I am forever grateful for those "slumming" sessions between writing where we indulged in Netflix binges, keeping my sanity intact. Jaypee, my right-hand man, you are the lighthouse that illuminates my path toward greater liberation and self-exploration, and for that, I am infinitely indebted to you.

To my friends, especially my squad—Tebs, Jess, Auntie Viv, Aïda—this is my love letter to our enduring friendship. Thank you for always pouring your love into me, even when I have little to give in return. My love for you all knows no bounds. Noam, thank you for always donning your cape every time I need a savior to remind me of my own capacity to save myself.

To Mom and Wonga, my pillars of strength, thank you for

your unyielding love and care. I am who I am today because of you, and everything I do is a reflection of that.

To all my incredible mentors, beloved well-wishers, and esteemed colleagues, you know exactly who you are. My heart swells with gratitude at the mere thought of you, for I believe that if I could embody even a fraction of the grace, kindness, and generosity you've shown me over the years, I would consider my life well lived.

Finally, I must give credit to my one and only good finger, the miraculous instrument through which this entire memoir was penned. The sheer audacity of writing an entire book on an iPhone with one finger is an accomplishment that engaged my entire being, an experiment in crip phenomenology.

And so, with my champagne raised high, I raise a toast to all of you. Here's to you, my dear ones! Cheers!